BIBLE WOMEN

BIBLE WOMEN

God's Word Speaks Today on Issues Facing Women in Africa

Gail Ekanem

Africa Christian Textbooks
2012

Bible Women: God's Word speaks Today on Issues Facing Women in Africa

© 2012 Gail Ekanem

ISBN: 978 905 160 1

Africa Christian Textbooks (ACTS)
ACTS Bookshop, International HQ, TCNN,
PMB 2020, Bukuru, Plateau State, 930008, Nigeria
GSM: +234 (0) 803-589-5328; E-mail: pa@actsnigeria.org
Website: http://actsnigeria.org

It is high time for women

to let their lights shine;

to bring their talents

that have been hidden

away rusting, and use

them for the glory of God,

and do with their might

what their hands find to do;

trusting God for strength,

who has said.

"I will never leave you or forsake you."[1]

Maria Woodworth Etter

Dedication

This book is dedicated to two wonderful Nigerian women, who are cherished friends and commendable examples of women who walk with God in the good times and the bad times.

Deaconess Comfort Essien of Etinan, in Akwa Ibom State. She has been a solid rock in my life since I met her many years ago in Belfast and then when I came to serve God among her people in Akwa Ibom State.

Deaconess Dinah Ekele of Odogomu, Kogi State, who has become a very dear and real friend, since the time I arrived as a stranger to Kogi State in 2006.

Both of these women have been influential in my life as prayer warriors and women of faith.

Abbreviations Used in This Book

(Unless otherwise indicated, Scripture quotations in this publication are from the Holy Bible, New International Version)

NIV = New International Version

ESV = English Standard Version

NLT = New Living Translation

TLB = The Living Bible

MSG= The Message

Gen. = Genesis

Ex. = Exodus

Lev. = Leviticus

Num. = Numbers

Deut. = Deuteronomy

Josh. = Joshua

Judg. = Judges

Ruth = Ruth

1 Sam. = 1 Samuel

2 Sam. = 2 Samuel

1 Kings = 1 Kings

2 Kings = 2 Kings

1 Chron. = 1 Chronicles

2 Chron. = 2 Chronicles

Ezra = Ezra

Neh. = Nehemiah

Est. = Esther

Job = Job

Ps. = Psalms

Prov. = Proverbs

Eccles. = Ecclesiastes

Song = Song of Songs

Isa. = Isaiah

Jer. = Jeremiah

Lam. = Lamentations

Ezek. = Ezekiel

Dan. = Daniel

Hos. = Hosea

Joel = Joel

Amos = Amos

Obad. = Obadiah

Jonah = Jonah

Mic. = Micah

Nah. = Nahum

Hab. = Habakkuk

Zeph. = Zephaniah

Hag. = Haggai

Zech. = Zechariah

Mal. = Malachi

Matt. = Matthew

Mark = Mark

Luke = Luke

John = John

Acts = Acts

Rom. = Romans

1 Cor. = 1 Corinthians

2 Cor. = 2 Corinthians

Gal. = Galatians

Eph. = Ephesians

Phil. = Philippians

Col. = Colossians

1 Thess. = 1 Thessalonians

2 Thess. = 2 Thessalonians

1 Tim. = 1 Timothy

2 Tim. = 2 Timothy

Titus = Titus

Philem. = Philemon

Heb. = Hebrews

James = James

1 Pet. = 1 Peter

2 Pet. = 2 Peter

1 John = 1 John

2 John = 2 John

3 John = 3 John

Jude = Jude

Rev.= Revelation

Table of Contents

Acknowledgements

I am very grateful to all those who helped in the production of this book.

I wish to begin by thanking my husband Godwin whose insights and corrections have been much valued.

Thanks go to Rev. John Enyinnaya and Rev. Samuel Ebukiba who both took time to read this and affirm that it might actually be of benefit to people in Africa.

Many thanks also go to Gloria Kearney who painstakingly corrected many errors and provided some very useful feedback from her acclaimed background in writing.

Pat Martin deserves much praise for completing the final proof reading before it left my hands to be published by ACTS.

Rev. Dr. Sid Garland (ACTS) has made some very valuable comments and has suggested ways of making the text more useful to a wider audience. Dr. Paul Todd has been instrumental in getting this book to its final stages. Thank you for your patience and attention to detail!

"My heart is stirred by a noble theme as I recite my verses for the king; my tongue is the pen of a skilful writer." (Ps. 45:1)

Introduction

The seed for this book began with the vision of including more women in our teaching programmes at Peter Achimugu College of Theology (PACT), Kogi State, Nigeria. It was something I was very excited about and in preparation, I began to examine the lives of some of the women mentioned in the Bible. My studies opened my eyes to the fact that many of their stories lend themselves very naturally as springboards to talk about particular issues that affect women in our society.

Jesus ministered to the lowly of society, the outcasts and the despised, and elevated them. He interacted with women, who in their day were relegated to the background holding little status in their society.[2]

> As their Creator, Jesus treated women as intrinsically valuable; he respected them as intelligent and faithful, and as disciples and labourers along with men.[3]

As we follow Jesus' example, we ought to be concerned for women who often continue to live under oppression and continue to be treated as second-class citizens. Jesus came to set the captives free, and the aim of this book is to see women set free by the truth of God's word.

God's word is a "lamp to my feet and a light for my path." (Ps. 119:105) As women of God, we look to the Scriptures to find out what it is that God wants to say to us. As we look particularly at the women in the Bible, it provides us with models of how to live and how not to live our lives for God. As we look at the lives of the women of the Bible, we will find things that will encourage, things that will be a warning for us, things that will spur us on to greater heights and even things that will challenge our perspective.

It is hoped that this book might be a useful resource in highlighting some of the pressing issues that face women in many African societies in particular and provide some godly perspectives on these matters.

Two particular questions will be asked about each of the characters studied.

What can we learn from the lives of the women of the Bible?

What can we learn about God?

I have not provided all the answers but have suggested some, leaving room for those who interact with the Biblical text to come up with some insights of their own. For this reason, I have added some further ideas to stimulate discussion and to motivate action.

I pray that as women in particular get their hands on this book, they will be greatly encouraged and will rise up to serve God with passion and courage.

The door of the classroom has not yet opened wide enough, so I have decided to bring the classroom to you. May you really be blessed!

Chapter One
Sarah – A Woman Who Waited

(Ref: Gen. 11:27-23:19; Isa. 51:2; Rom. 4:19; 9:9;

Gal. 4:21-31; Heb. 11:11; 1 Pet. 3:5-6).

Name

Sarai means 'princess.' Sarah means 'mother of nations.'[4]

Profile

- Married to Abraham but was also his half-sister.

- Lived originally in Ur of the Chaldeans, until Abraham was called to move to Canaan.

- A wife, mother, and a household manager.

Background

Genesis is a book of beginnings. Through Abraham and Sarah God began the formation of a covenant people, a people of his very own. From this chosen nation would come the Saviour of the world.[5] God had a plan for their lives and despite various setbacks and impossible situations, God brought that plan into being. Through the chosen nation of Israel, all nations would be blessed. The story of Sarah centred on the promise of a son, and Isaac was born around 2066 B.C.[6]

What lessons can we learn from Sarah's life?

Sarah was:

A wife to a man on transfer

> The Lord had said to Abram, 'Leave your country,
> your people and your father's household and go to
> the land I will show you.' (Gen. 12:1)

"So Abram left, as the Lord had told him . . . He took his wife Sara . . . and they arrived there." (Gen. 12: 4-5)

Moving is not trouble-free. In fact, moving house or moving to a new location is one of the things in a person's life that can cause a high level of stress.

> Moving is no fun, particularly when your moving
> van is a camel or a donkey and especially when you
> don't even know where you are going.[7]

It is not always easy to move from place to place, but in response to God's command, Sarah loyally followed her husband wherever God called him. God's command overruled the inconveniences that Sarah might experience in the process.

Sometimes, it is not our own fault and circumstances such as a lack of finance may force husbands and wives to be apart, but it is not good for the relationship to spend too much time apart. It leaves the marriage vulnerable and open to attack by the enemy. Genesis 2:18 states "The Lord God said 'It is not good for the man to be alone. I will make a helper suitable for him.'" Husbands and wives are meant to be together, providing companionship and love to one another. Long periods of separation can put a great strain on the marriage relationship and can cause irreparable damage to the family unit. Sarah was committed to being wherever her partner was, whenever that was possible. *"What a happy and holy fashion it is that those who love one another should rest on the same pillow."*[8]

Beautiful

" . . . I know what a beautiful woman you are . . ." (Gen. 12:11)

Sarah was beautiful. It seems that Sarah was pretty to look at on the outside, but also was inwardly beautiful. Peter later on in the Bible uses Sarah as a model for feminine beauty.

> Your beauty should not come from outward adornment . . . Instead, it should be that of your inner self, the unfading beauty of a gentle and quiet spirit, which is of great worth in God's sight. For this is the way the holy women of the past who put their hope in God used to make themselves beautiful. They were submissive to their own husbands, like Sarah, who obeyed Abraham and called him her master. (1 Pet. 3:3-6)

Sarah's respect and her self-giving love to her husband made her beautiful. A woman may be physically beautiful but the way she conducts herself in her relationships also affects her beauty. Sarah called her husband 'lord' or 'master.' This was a term of respect in Sarah's day. In some African societies, wives do not address their husbands by their first name. The older generation sometimes call them 'Daddy' while the younger generation may refer to their spouse by using a pet name, for example, 'Precious.' It is good to remember that it is not the expression of the mouth that is really the important thing here, but an inner attitude of submission and obedience. Faith and submission go together. If we have faith that God will work through our husbands to accomplish what is best for us, then submission is easy, remembering also that cooperation works both ways. "Submit to one another out of reverence for Christ." (Eph. 5: 21)

Barren

"Now Sarai, Abram's wife had borne him no children." (Gen. 16: 1)

Sarah was barren or childless. In Sarah's day, a woman's social standing and security were linked with her ability to produce children and especially sons. In the culture of her day, people treated barren women with contempt. Fertility was a blessing, while barrenness was a curse. A woman who bore many sons received favour and respect from the society and was assured of a comfortable old age. It is similar even in many societies today. Women who are childless are looked down upon and often treated harshly. Sarah felt acutely the pain of not having a child. She perhaps waited monthly to see if her situation had changed. Then to make matters worse, she probably faced the many questions of others about her condition and knew her husband's keen disappointment. Sarah felt the shame, humility and disappointment of barrenness. Many childless women face a similar situation today. So how did she handle it? Not very well, it seems.

Mistaken in thinking she could solve her own problem

> ... she had an Egyptian maidservant named Hagar; so she said to Abram, 'The LORD has kept me from having children. Go sleep with my maidservant; perhaps I can build a family through her.' (Gen. 16:1)

Sarah decided to take things into her own hands. She was influenced by society, instead of by God's ways. She blamed herself for her childlessness, though childlessness is not always the fault of the woman. It is important to note that the man can also be the cause of infertility problems.

Sarah decided to achieve motherhood through a household slave. This was a common practice in the society of her day but was not God's design for marriage. (Matt. 19:4-6) Sarah gave Hagar to Abraham and she conceived and bore a son, called Ishmael. However, Sarah's decision to achieve motherhood in this way did not turn out well. By following her own plan, she brought discord and tension into her home. Sarah became jealous of Hagar and even blamed Abraham for the problem she herself had caused.

> Then Sarai said to Abram, 'You are responsible for the wrong I am suffering. I put my servant in your arms, and now that she knows she is pregnant, she despises me. May the LORD judge between you and me. (Gen. 16:5)

Sarah thought this was the perfect solution to her dilemma, but it was not so perfect after all, as her servant began to despise her. "There is a way that seems right to a man, but in the end it leads to death." (Prov. 14:12) In the ancient Near East a surrogate marriage, whereby a slave girl bore a child for her mistress was Sarah's preferred option. Yet the narrator highlights the fact three times in two verses that "Hagar bore Abram a son." (Gen. 16:15-16) Sarah gained nothing by her own efforts, for she still had no child to call her own.[9]

Though Sarah's decision was an unwise one, we can understand her reasons for acting as she did. The barren woman faces the stigma of barrenness and bears the shame that comes from the societal view of barrenness. Her attempts at achieving pregnancy leave her feeling disappointed and scared that her marriage is in trouble. She spends each day worrying about the insecurity of her marriage and the possibility that the husband might take another wife into the marital home. Other people's questions and insensitivity can leave the woman feeling inadequate and believing that she has not fulfilled her role in life.

Family members can put extreme pressure on the woman to get pregnant, by any means. In some tribes, the wife is not even accepted as a wife until she has a child and only when she has a male child does a wife really feel secure in her marital home. For some couples, the whole purpose of marriage is to have children to continue the family line. If this does not happen, then much strain is put on the relationship.

Both partners may be tempted to get involved in extra marital affairs for the purpose of proving their fertility and bearing a child. Some may even pay money to juju men who offer sacrifices to the spirits in an attempt to secure a pregnancy. However, whose power is greater, that of God or that of the juju man?

> 'To whom will you compare me? Or who is my
> equal?' says the Holy One. 'Lift your eyes and look
> to the heavens: Who created all these? He who

brings out the starry host one by one, and calls them each by name. Because of his great power and mighty strength not one of them is missing.' (Isa. 40:25-26)

Certainly, children are part of God's plan for marriage, but marriage can exist without children, as God's primary purpose for marriage is companionship.

Then the LORD God said, 'It is not good for the man to be alone; I will make him a helper who is just right for him.' (Gen. 2: 18 NLT)

On one occasion when Jesus was teaching, a woman from the crowd called out "Blessed is the mother who gave you birth and nursed you." (Luke 11:27) Jesus' response to her declaration is an interesting one. He said "'Blessed rather are those who hear the word of God and obey it.'" (Luke 11:28) In other words, Jesus believes that there is something more honourable than to give birth to human life. Jesus proclaims that greater honour is to be given to the one who hears God's life-giving word and puts it into practice. Jesus speaks at a time and in a culture where the woman's primary function in life was to bear children. A woman's value was associated with how many sons she bore. Jesus is letting women know here, that they are not just baby-making machines. God expects something else from them. They are to learn God's word and to put it into practice. As important as bearing children is, there is something more important, something more essential, that is, hearing and obeying God's word.

Full of doubt

> Then the Lord said to Abraham, 'Why did Sarah laugh and say, 'Will I really have a child now that I am old?' 'Is anything too hard for the LORD?' (Gen. 18: 13-14)

Sarah had a problem with doubt. She had heard God's promise to Abraham that he would have a son, but she was not seeing the answer through her own body. Let us not be quick to condemn her as she was by now ninety years of age. It certainly was not easy to believe that it could happen at this stage, especially in the case of a woman who had been barren all her married life. Nevertheless, Sarah should have remembered that God could do immeasurably more than all she could have asked or imagined. (Eph. 3:20) In some societies, the practice is often to consult witch doctors or herbalists, rather than trust wholly in God. By consulting such people, we deny God's power to act on our behalf.

Whether we have or do not have children lies outside our control but is determined by God. Psalm 127: 3 states "Sons are a heritage from the Lord, children a reward from him." Many women make the same mistake that Sarah made. We can allow the problem of barrenness to become a cause of disagreement in our marriage or we can continue to trust in God's perfect promises and timing. God does not need our help to fulfil his promise. He hears the cries of our hearts and knows what we need.

Victorious at last

> Now the Lord was gracious to Sarah as he had said,
> and the Lord did for Sarah what he had promised.
> Sarah became pregnant and bore a son to Abraham
> in his old age, at the very time God had promised
> him. (Gen. 21:1-2)

Sarah was the first of many who faced the same problem. Others included Rebekah, Rachel, and Hannah. Each of these women responded to their situations differently, but in the end, each of them gave birth to a child. In all of these scenarios, prayer seems to have been the key to success.

Rebekah and Isaac certainly in the early years enjoyed a close intimate relationship.

> Isaac brought her into the tent of his mother, Sarah,
> and he married Rebekah. So she became his wife,
> and he loved her; and Isaac was comforted after his
> mother's death. (Gen. 24:67)

Despite the joy and closeness of their relationship, there was no sign of children and there is no doubt that it was a matter of distress to them. They had been married for twenty years and they had no success in having children. Isaac had not abandoned his wife because of it. He loved her and responded to the situation with wisdom.

> Isaac prayed to the Lord on behalf of his wife,
> because she was barren. The LORD answered his
> prayer and his wife Rebekah became pregnant.
> (Gen. 25:21)

Rachel was also childless. Rachel had the added complication of being in competition with her sister Leah for Jacob's affections, though there was no uncertainty of Jacob's love for her. She was his favourite. It was difficult though for Rachel to watch Leah give birth to Jacob's children, while she remained barren. It was not easy, and Rachel poured out her annoyance upon her husband.

> When Rachel saw that she was not bearing Jacob
> any children, she became jealous of her sister. So she

said to Jacob, 'Give me children, or I'll die!' (Gen. 30:1).

Both her reaction of jealousy towards her sister and her anger towards her husband did not help her situation. Her husband responded equally with agitation. "Am I in the place of God, who has kept you from having children?" (Gen. 30:2).

Couples facing childlessness often blame each other and allow the stress of childlessness to sour their relationship. We need to guard against this. God instituted marriage for relieving loneliness. Wives are primarily companions and friends to their husbands. Their primary purpose is not to be a baby-making machine.

God is in control, and he is a good and wise God, so sometimes we need to remind ourselves that he knows what is best for us. Rachel did not accept her childlessness with ease. She became obsessed with having children, no matter what. She looked at what she did not have, and it began to spoil even the good things that she did have. It put a strain on her marriage, but God still was gracious to her, despite her wrong reactions. At the right time, "God remembered Rachel; he listened to her and opened her womb." (Gen. 30:22)

Hannah found herself in a similar situation. She was childless and, in her case, she had a further burden to bear because her husband had a second wife, who was very unsympathetic to her predicament. Peninnah, the second wife took every opportunity to remind Hannah of her inadequacy.

> And because the LORD had closed her womb, her rival kept provoking her in order to irritate her. This went on year after year. Whenever Hannah went up to the house of the LORD, her rival provoked her till she wept and would not eat. (1 Sam. 1:6-7)

Hannah suffered terribly at the hands of her insensitive and heartless rival. I wonder how it would have been if circumstances were reversed? For Hannah the pain of her tragic situation was unbearable. She poured out her great sorrow to God, which is a wise practice for all of us to emulate. At the right time, "Elkanah lay with Hannah his wife, and the LORD remembered her." (1 Sam. 1:19)

God is good and his timing is perfect. Answers to prayer can be slow, but they come. When we hold on to faith, it will result in joy. Sarah laughed earlier with incredulity, at the declaration that she would become a mother in her old age, but now she laughed with joy as Isaac is born.

> Sarah said, 'God has brought me laughter, and everyone who hears about this will laugh with me.' And she added, 'Who would have said to Abraham that Sarah would nurse children? Yet I have borne him a son in his old age.' (Gen. 21:6-7)

God has not forgotten you. Remember that your value and dignity come from God. You are his child and are precious to him. Your worth does not come from the amount of children you have, though culture might say differently. God's word is greater than cultural expectations! What God requires of us is a close and intimate walk with him wherever he leads us.

> He has showed you, O man, what is good. And what does the LORD require of you? To act justly and to love mercy and to walk humbly with your God. (Mic. 6:8)

What lessons can we learn about God?

God is:

A promise-keeping God

> . . . You know with all your heart and soul that not one of all the good promises the LORD your God gave you has failed. (Josh. 23:14, see also Num. 23:19)

If God has really made a promise to us, we can trust him. He is not like man who may promise but fail, for many reasons, to fulfil that promise. God is completely dependable and can be trusted! He will do what he has said he will do.

A God of perfect timing

> But do not forget this one thing, dear friends: with the Lord a day is like a thousand years, and a thousand years are like a day. (2 Pet. 3:8)

Sometimes we get impatient as we wait for God to answer our prayers. What appears like a delay can be God's perfect timing. God may have other things he wants to develop in us before we are ready for what we so earnestly desire. Wait for him.

Gracious to us even when we fail miserably

> And he passed in front of Moses, proclaiming, 'The LORD, the LORD, the compassionate and gracious

> God, slow to anger, abounding in love and
> faithfulness, maintaining love to thousands, and
> forgiving wickedness, rebellion and sin. (Ex. 34:6)

God continued to fulfil his promise to Sarah, despite her doubts. What he has done for others, he can do for us. God knows what we are like and still loves us.

Able to do immeasurably more than all we can ask or imagine

> Now to him who is able to do immeasurably more
> than all we ask or imagine, according to his power
> that is at work within us, to him be glory in the
> church and in Christ Jesus throughout all
> generations, for ever and ever! Amen. (Eph. 3:20-21)

God answers our prayers abundantly. Hannah prayed for a son, but God gave her four sons and two daughters. (1 Sam. 2:31) What seems impossible for us is possible for God. Sarah's old age was not a problem for God. Nothing is too difficult for him. He makes a way where there is no way!

Sovereign

> But as for me. It is good to be near God. I have made
> the Sovereign LORD my refuge; I will tell of all your
> deeds. (Ps. 73:28)

God is in charge, and nothing can thwart his purpose or plan for our lives. If he does not give children, he has good reasons for doing so. He is not a cruel God but works all situations together for good.

> And we know that in all things God works for the
> good of those who love him, who have been called
> according to his purpose. (Rom. 8:28)

God is the Sovereign LORD and knows what he is doing.

Special Focus: Christ in the Story of Sarah

Sarah's story centres round the promise of a son. The birth of Isaac was the beginning of God's promise and plan to save mankind. Through Abraham, all men would be blessed, (Gen. 12:3) because from Abraham's seed and line the Saviour of the world would come. Jesus Christ, the descendant of Abraham was born in a stable in Bethlehem.

> And the Word became flesh and dwelt among us
> and we have seen his glory, glory as of the only Son
> from the Father full of grace and truth. (John 1:14)

God became man and made his dwelling among us, so that we might be saved.

> For God so loved the world that he gave his one and only Son, that whoever believes in him shall not perish but have eternal life. (John 3:16)

Through Abraham's line, the Promised Son, who would take away the sins of the world, was born.

> Whoever believes in him is not condemned, but whoever does not believe stands condemned already because he does not believe in the name of God's one and only Son. (John 3:18)

Do you believe in Jesus, God's one and only Son?

For Further Discussion

1. What situation have you faced or are you facing in your life that requires you to hold on to God with faith and trust?

2. Think about times in your life when you have tried to 'help' God, rather than allow him to answer your prayers in his way and in his time. Discuss the result.

3. What can you do to encourage other women to handle better some of the difficult issues of life, like childlessness?

Chapter Two
Deborah–A Woman Who Led

(Ref: Judges 4 & 5)

Name

Deborah means 'bee' or might possibly mean 'spirited or fiery woman.'[10]

Profile

- Lived in Canaan.

- A prophetess and a judge.

- Married to Lappidoth.

Background

God's covenant people had been brought into the Promised Land by Joshua, though much of the land still needed to be conquered. Joshua had since died, and God raised up a series of judges to rule Israel. The book of Judges follows a cyclical pattern of disobedience, oppression, repentance, and restoration. The people sinned by turning away from God which resulted in judgement. Under their enemies' oppression, the people cried out to God once more and God graciously sent a deliverer in the form of a judge. Deborah is one of such judges raised up to deliver God's people and provide leadership. Deborah's story takes place around 1209 B.C.[11]

What lessons can we learn from Deborah's Life?

Deborah was:

A prophetess

"Deborah, a prophetess, the wife of Lappidoth, was leading Israel at that time." (Judg. 4:4)

The first thing mentioned about Deborah is that she was a prophetess. Some other prophetesses mentioned in the Bible are Anna (Luke 2:36-37) and the four daughters of Philip. (Acts 21:8-9) A prophetess is a woman who has been called by God to speak his message to others and Deborah was one of such women entrusted by God to speak his message to the nation of Israel. Therefore, it is clear that God is happy to use women as his messengers. God calls women and gives them his authority to speak to others on his behalf. Remember the promise of God through the prophet Joel.

> I will pour out my Spirit on all people. Your sons and daughters will prophesy, your old men will dream dreams, your young men will see visions. Even on my servants, both men and women, I will pour out my Spirit in those days. (Joel 2:28)

If God has called you to be a prophetess, then Deborah is a good example for you to follow. Deborah heard from God and spoke God's word to God's people. God gave wisdom and instruction to Deborah, which enabled her to rule her people effectively. God also gave Deborah details of the tactics and military strategy that Israel should use in gaining victory over her adversaries. Deborah was a true prophetess who heard God's word and had the courage to put it into practice.

Deborah was a mouthpiece for God. She was close to God and gained wisdom from God. She listened and heard from God and communicated God's will to Barak the military general.

> The Lord, the God of Israel, commands you: Go take with you ten thousand men of Naphtali and Zebulun and lead the way to Mount Tabor. I will

> lure Sisera, the commander of Jabin's army, with his
> chariots and his troops to the Kishon River and give
> him into your hands. (Judg. 4:6-7)

Deborah trusted and had every confidence in God's word. She communicated God's word to others, while at the same time she represented the people before God. Deborah, like other good prophets urged the people to obey God.

There are some women in the Church who claim to be prophetesses, but not everyone who claims to be a prophetess is God's appointed servant. God's word is clear in stating that false prophets and prophetesses may operate within the Church.

> For false Christs and false prophets will appear and
> perform signs and miracles to deceive the elect–if
> that were possible. (Mark 13:22)

"But there were also false prophets among the people, just as there will be false teachers among you." (2 Pet. 2:1) Therefore, we need to be on guard and discern truth from falsehood. There are some prophets and prophetesses in our time who do not hear the voice of God but speak from their own imaginings. They have not entered into the counsel of God and neither has God sent them with a message. "They speak visions from their own minds, not from the mouth of the LORD." (Jer. 23:16)

Prophecy is to be tested. "Two or three prophets should speak, and the others should weigh carefully what is said." (1 Cor. 14: 29) Prophecy is not to be swallowed hook, line and sinker, but is to be examined with care. The following questions may be useful in testing prophecy:

- Is it in line with God's character and word?

- Does the prophecy draw you closer to God or further away from God?

- Does the prophecy produce discord, disunity, and havoc or does it build up the Church?

> But everyone who prophesies speaks to men **for their strengthening, encouragement, and comfort.** He who speaks in a tongue edifies himself, but he who prophesies **edifies the Church**. (1 Cor. 14:3-4 own emphasis)

A false prophet bears bad fruit. " . . . by their fruit you will recognise them . . ." (Matt. 7:15-17) Too often, the words of false prophets are not challenged and cause untold damage in our churches and communities.

A wife

Deborah was married. Apart from the mention of Lappidoth here, Deborah's husband appears to fade into the background. Deborah is the key figure or prominent person. Some men find it difficult to accept a situation where it appears that the woman is in the forefront, while the man remains in the background. In some places, women are killed because their talents and gifts have caused them to overshadow their husbands. Lappidoth goes down in the annals of history as simply Deborah's husband. He appears to accept his wife's calling and has not hindered her role as God's chosen leader in Israel. Lappidoth does not appear to have stood in the way of this gifted lady. Deborah's role and responsibilities as a wife also do not obstruct her from following God's special calling into leadership.

A leader of Israel

There are no explanations as to why Deborah was the leader of Israel, though many today may voice their suggestions. In the Scriptures, it is simply stated that Deborah was "leading Israel at that time." (Judg. 4:4) It does not appear here that any explanation is necessary. God obviously did not see Deborah's role as leader over

Israel as inappropriate. Deborah was a good leader who knew how to delegate, how to plan and how to skilfully direct others. Deborah knew God called her and her authority to rule came from God. Her motherly concern for her people and her heart of courage made her an effective leader. "Village life in Israel ceased, ceased until I, Deborah, arose, arose a mother in Israel." (Judg. 5:7)

When Deborah began to rule, the situation of Israel was a desperate one. The nation had faced the wrath and oppression of Jabin for over twenty years.

> Because he had nine hundred iron chariots and had cruelly oppressed the Israelites for twenty years, they cried to the LORD for help. (Judg. 4:3)

What does God do? He sends a woman—an unexpected move that surprises us. As Wilcock suggests *"God keeps his promises as to what he will do, but that we cannot tie him down as to how he will do it."*[12] God's solution to this particular situation is a woman. God bestowed leadership upon this woman and placed her in the right place, at the right time. Deborah goes down in history as a great example of godly leadership, for other women to imitate.

The book of Judges records a time in Israel's history when they were experiencing a failure of community and an attitude of each man for himself, instead of living, working and supporting one another in community. Deborah was instrumental in changing the course of history. Before the arrival of Deborah, the enemy had the upper hand, but in her time, she was able to restore the people's security. The people had lived under oppression for twenty years. They had become a helpless nation living in fear, because of the lawless society, too afraid even to travel on the main roads. The odds were stacked against Israel, but they succeeded. The important thing about Deborah is not so much her gender, as much as the fact that God chose her for this role. Following her time as leader, "the land had peace for forty years." (Judg. 5:31) Deborah left behind a legacy of peace. Under her leadership, the people she served enjoyed peace and security and the restoration of a faithful relationship with God.

A wise judge

> She held court under the Palm of Deborah between Ramah and Bethel in the hill country of Ephraim, and the Israelites came to her to have their disputes decided. (Judg. 4:5)

A judge was an individual, who served as a political, military, and spiritual leader in Israel. The people accepted Deborah's leadership. The shade of the palm tree was her courthouse where she deliberated and issued her verdicts on the matters presented before her. The people of Israel came to her for her wise judgement and Deborah mediated disputes and was concerned to bring order and justice to her people's lives. She was a wise woman like the woman of noble virtue in Proverbs 31: 26 "She speaks with wisdom and faithful instruction is on her tongue." She was a true shepherd who was concerned about her flock and her godly wisdom drew people to her. Deborah was a notable leader who was concerned for her people and was not obsessed with gaining popularity and worldly success.

It seems that Deborah was the best person for the job and the fact that she was a woman did not mean she could not take up the position. She was the only female judge, amongst those chosen by God. God chose her to lead Israel and he does not make mistakes. Deborah did not allow her culture or her position as a wife to hinder her from serving God in this special way. " . . .in her weakness in a patriarchal world, Deborah proves to be God's answer."[13]

A woman of courage

"Very well, Deborah said, I will go with you." (Judg. 4: 9)

Barak needed Deborah's presence on the battlefield and Deborah agreed to accompany him. She was a motivator who instilled courage in others. Without her, Barak would not have faced the battle. Deborah's willingness and courage to follow God wholeheartedly stands in stark contrast to Barak's reluctance to trust God.

Deborah reminds us very much of David, who as a boy went to visit his brothers on the battlefield, only to find all of Israel cowering in fear before Goliath and the Philistines. (1 Sam. 17: 11, 24) David could not understand such behaviour, in light of the fact that the army of Israel belonged to God Almighty. David's response to Goliath was different to that of his fellow Israelites as seen by his question, "Who is this uncircumcised Philistine that he should defy the armies of the living God?" (1 Sam. 17:26) Deborah also found her help in God. She was a godly woman who looked to God as her help.

Deborah had David's kind of faith. She was not afraid to march into battle alongside the army of Israel. Deborah feared God and not man. "He who fears the LORD has a secure fortress." (Prov. 14:26) "Fear of man will prove to be a snare, but whoever trusts in the LORD is kept safe." (Prov. 29:25)

Deborah did not trust in Israel's weapons or indeed the lack of them in the face of the Canaanite's arsenal of sophisticated weapons. If one's eyes were on the military might of the Canaanites, then they should have won the battle but they did not. Deborah's trust lay in her God and the Israelites won the battle despite how things appeared. God overcame Israel's enemy by allowing a flash flood to turn the battleground into a field of mud. The metal chariots on which the Canaanites depended were soon bogged down in the mud and proved to be a hindrance rather than a help. Ironically, the Canaanite god Baal was the god of storms and God used a storm to hinder this great army! Let us remember that God is the Almighty God who has assured us of his constant presence and help. Let us rise up to be women of courage like Deborah.

A woman of vision

> Then Deborah said to Barak, 'Go! This is the day that the LORD has given Sisera into your hands. Has not the LORD gone ahead of you?' (Judg. 4:14)

Deborah was able to look beyond the present terrible circumstances that Israel faced to take hold of God's promise of victory. If God had assured them of victory, then as far as Deborah was concerned it was certain—it would surely happen! Someone once said, *"People of vision see the invisible, hear the inaudible, believe the incredible, think the unthinkable and do the impossible."*

A worshipper of God

"On that day Deborah and Barak son of Abinoam sang this song." (Judg. 5:1)

> God commanded Deborah to wake up and sing and Barak to wake up and attack the enemy. Because of her faith, Deborah could sing before the battle started as well as after the battle ended.[14]

When the battle was over, Deborah sang praises to her God, in acknowledgement of his faithfulness throughout. She was aware that God had secured the victory for Israel. As she heard God's word and put it into practice, God granted success to Israel's mission and Deborah responded to God's action with praise.

Israel's achievement of victory was important as it opened up the fertile Plain of Esdraelon and parts of the Plain of Sharon to the Israelites[15] and Deborah was quick to give the glory for this victory to God. She lived a life that glorified God. Her actions and judgements pointed to God and not away from him, and she led others to honour and worship Him. "Hear O kings; give ear O princes; to the LORD I will sing; I will make melody to the LORD, the God of Israel." (Judg. 5:3 ESV)

> To the sound of the musicians at the watering places, there they repeat the righteous triumphs of the LORD, the righteous triumphs of his villagers in Israel. (Judg. 5:11 ESV)

A team player

Deborah was a woman of many talents and abilities, but she knew she could not do the work alone. She was happy to be a team player. She worked as part of a team to accomplish the task of saving Israel from their Canaanite oppressors. The task was certainly not an easy one, but together with God's help victory became theirs. Many of the tribes followed her leadership and together victory was made possible. "When the princes in Israel take the lead, when the people willingly offer themselves- praise the LORD!" (Judg. 5:2). There are things that we can accomplish together that we could not do on our own.

A woman who made a difference

Many societies generally still believe that the woman's place is in the home. Establishing a godly home and training children is a vital role to play, but God asked something different of Deborah. She was to take up the role of leadership, making important decisions for the good of her nation. She made wise judgements on cases that troubled her people. Her gender did not prohibit her from taking such a role and her strength for the task came from the Lord.

Deborah stood out from the crowd. As "everyone did what was right in his own eyes," Deborah walked in step with her Master, listening for his voice and following his commands. Deborah knew whom she followed. God had drawn her to himself and called her to a post of great responsibility. She was open to her Master's call and yielded her life to him. She was willing to go when God said, *'Go!'* Deborah depended upon the Lord of Hosts and she became a woman who made a difference. You too can become a godly woman who can be used by God to make a difference.

What lessons can we learn about God?

God is:

A warrior

"On that day God subdued Jabin, the Canaanite king, before the Israelites." (Judg. 4:23) God is the one who provided the strategy for the battle. Barak had merely to show up and God would hand the enemy over to him. God is the one credited with the victory over the Canaanite King, Jabin.

Powerful

"Once God has spoken; twice have I heard this: that power belongs to God." (Ps. 62:11) All power belongs to God and no human might or power can stand against him. Despite the obvious power of the Canaanites with their sophisticated weapons, God overcame them. God demonstrated his control over the weather and used it to defeat his enemies. He intervened and turned around the obvious prowess and strength of the Canaanites to weakness and miraculously gave his ill-equipped people the victory.

Compassionate and merciful despite his people's waywardness

> For the LORD your God is a merciful God; he will
> not abandon or destroy you or forget the covenant
> with your forefathers, which he confirmed to them
> by oath. (Deut. 4:31)

Repeatedly the Israelites fell into the trap of forgetting God. This began a cycle of oppression at the hands of an enemy nation, which was followed by penitence. God looked with mercy on his people and lovingly provided deliverance for his people in the form of a judge. God knows the mess we can get ourselves in and when we cry out to him, He rescues us.

Wise

"For the foolishness of God is wiser than man's wisdom, and the weakness of God is stronger than man's strength." (1 Cor. 1:25) God shows his wisdom in choosing the right person for the job. God did not make a mistake when he chose Deborah but entrusted her with the privilege of serving his people as judge and leader. God does not discriminate based on gender or race. He sees everyone the same and uses women in his work as well as men. In this instance, Deborah was *"the chosen light of God in a dark world."*[16]

Special Focus: Christ in the Story of Deborah

Deborah as a deliverer of her people foreshadows Christ who came as the perfect Deliverer of all mankind. Romans 11:26 records

> . . . The Deliverer will come from Zion, he will banish ungodliness from Jacob; and this will be my covenant with them when I take away their sins. (ESV)

The people in Deborah's day could not save themselves. They required help from outside. Indeed, they required God's intervention. Psalm 3:8 records "From the LORD comes deliverance." We are no different and need outside help and intervention if we are to be saved. For us, God the Father has provided the perfect Deliverer in his son Jesus Christ, who did for us what we could not do for ourselves. Christ delivers us from sin, evil and the coming wrath. (See Matt. 1:21; Gal. 1:3-4; Rom. 5:9)

Much like Deborah, Christ was an unexpected Deliverer. The religious leaders and others found it hard to recognise Jesus as the Promised Deliverer for he was not what they expected. They anticipated a powerful king who by his might and power would overthrow the oppressive rule of Rome. Instead, they got a humble teacher and healer who died on a cross.

There is a Judge over all the earth. Judges like Deborah only secured peace among the people for a time. Perfect peace will only be ours when Christ's perfect rule comes. Is Christ your Prince of Peace?

For Further Discussion

1. Look up the following verses. 1 Cor. 14:29; 1 John 4:1. In light of these verses why is it important to test prophecy and how can we effectively test it?

2. Why is teamwork important in building God's kingdom?

3. Deborah was courageous and performed the task that God called her to do. In doing so, she made a difference. Are there ways in which you feel God prompting you to make a difference?

Chapter Three
Ruth–A Woman Who Was Loyal

(Ref: Ruth 1- 4; Matt. 1:5)

Name

Ruth means 'a lovely friend.'[17]

Profile

- A foreign woman from Moab that is, a Moabitess.

- Was married to an Israelite, named Mahlon, son of Elimelech and Naomi.

- Now a destitute widow.

Background

The story of Ruth is set in the time after the judges, a time of disobedience and of turning away from God. Even in such times, there were those who demonstrated faith in God. What is remarkable about Ruth is that she was a foreigner, who loved the God of Israel. While the Israelites turned their back on God, Ruth turned to him in faith. Her story takes place sometime between 1375 and 1050 B.C.[18]

What lessons can we learn from Ruth's life?

Ruth was:

A foreigner

> Now Elimelech, Naomi's husband died, and she was left with her two sons. They married Moabite women, one named Orpah and the other Ruth. (Ruth 1:3-4a)

Ruth was originally a Moabitess, that is, from Moab. The Israelites looked upon the Moabites as inferior to them. Moab was the son of Lot's eldest daughter and was the result of the night that Lot's daughters had made their father drunk and slept with him. (Gen. 19:30-38) The Moabites were the descendants of Moab. (Gen. 19:37) Besides their far from perfect origin, the Moabites had developed a less than perfect relationship with Israel. They had failed to come to the aid of Israel when the nation of Israel was fleeing from Egypt. To add insult to injury, the people of Moab had hired Balaam to proclaim a curse over Israel. (Deut. 23:3-6). The Moabites were enemies of Israel, which makes the story of Ruth all the more remarkable.

Ruth married from amongst her enemies. Yet ironically, this foreigner and enemy of Israel became loyal to Israel's God, refused to follow the ways of her fathers, while in contrast many Israelites had turned their backs on God, and given their hearts to the worship of the gods of Moab.

> Again, the Israelites did evil in the eyes of the LORD. They served the Baals and the Ashtoreths, and the gods of Aram, the gods of Sidon, the gods of Moab, the gods of the Ammonites and the gods of the Philistines. (Judg. 10:6)

One of the main gods of Moab was Chemosh. Child sacrifice was often associated with the worship of Chemosh. So the Israelites engaged in this worship, which was abominable in God's sight. In contrast, the story of Ruth tells of a young Moabite woman, a foreigner who rejected the gods of her own people and submitted to the God of Israel.

A widow

> After they had lived there about ten years, both Mahlon and Kilion also died, and Naomi was left without her two sons and her husband. (Ruth 1:4-5)

The literal meaning of the Hebrew word for widow is *'a desolate place'*[19] or *'an empty house.'*[20] Ruth found herself after ten years of marriage facing the burden of the great loss of her partner in life. Not only that, her father-in-law and brother-in-law had also died. If that was not enough, she had remained childless despite her marriage of ten years. Life had dealt Ruth a bitter blow. The breadwinners of the family were gone. She had no children and her future looked bleak.

Some women become widows at an early age due to fatal accidents, communal clashes and various diseases. Overnight, women can find themselves in extreme hardship, facing terrible psychological trauma. It is particularly traumatic for the childless widow. Such widows may face extreme discrimination and in some cases are treated as non-persons. They can be left bereft, without house and home, penniless and shunned. A widow faces the possibility of having everything that her husband owned grabbed by in-laws who feel that they have a greater right, being blood relatives of the deceased. Some widows also face ritual customs that are debasing and humiliating, for example having to scrape their hair off, being forced to drink water used to wash the corpse of the dead husband as a way of proving that they were not responsible for the death of their husband. On top of this, they are forced to swear oaths, and even persuaded to marry an in-law. Is this really happening today? Yes, it is in some places, and despite modern laws, widows' rights are often completely ignored.

However, all is not lost, and God is the Defender of widows. "A father to the fatherless, a defender of widows, is God in his holy dwelling. (Ps. 68:5) He hears their cries and will protect them.

> Do not take advantage of a widow or an orphan. If
> you do and they cry out to me, I will certainly hear
> their cry. (Ex. 22:22-23)

God sustains and watches out for the well-being of the widow.

> The LORD watches over the alien and sustains the
> fatherless and the widow, but he frustrates the ways
> of the wicked. (Ps. 146:9)

God expects his own people to reflect his concern for the vulnerable in society.

> Religion that God our father accepts as pure and
> faultless is this: to look after orphans and widows in
> their distress. (James 1:26)

The story of Ruth demonstrates God's care and concern for one particular vulnerable widow.

Loyal

> 'Don't urge me to leave you, or to turn back from you. Where you go, I will go, and where you stay, I will stay. Your people will be my people and your God my God.' (Ruth 1:16)

When tragedy strikes, Naomi makes every effort to urge both Orpah and Ruth to return to their homeland, so that they can again find security and a home with a new husband.

> The particular wish for their well-being is important in that it constitutes a desire for them to be remarried, a sign of the importance of male presence to these bereaved women.[21]

At this point, Orpah is persuaded and leaves the two widows, while Ruth remains with Naomi.

Ruth found herself in a tough situation. She was a childless widow. By making the choice to follow Naomi back to Israel, she would be particularly vulnerable as a foreign, childless woman. It may have been a difficult prospect, but Ruth knew that there was only one thing she could do. Ruth stood by her mother-in-law. Ruth graciously laid aside her own interests, sacrificing them in order to take care of Naomi. Obviously, a friendship had been forged between the two and Ruth was not prepared to give up on the old woman in her hour of need. She knew that Naomi and her God were worth holding on to. She knew not what lay ahead but chose to move forward with God into an unknown future. From the world's point of view, there was little apparent wisdom in Ruth going with Naomi.

Relationships move in two directions. Ruth loved and respected her mother-in-law and Naomi loved and cherished her daughter-in-law as if she was her own daughter. She advised her and was concerned for her well-being. She was willing to release her, feeling that it would be in Ruth's best interest to return to her own people. Naomi loved and took care of her daughter-in-law and Ruth drew near to this elderly, godly woman. God knit and bound these two lives together. They complemented each other and they lived together in a peaceful relationship. They were concerned enough to put each other's needs above their own. This mutual commitment to each other overshadowed any differences between them in terms of culture, age, and tribe. Naomi cared for Ruth and advised her, while Ruth cared for Naomi and worked to provide for them both.

Some daughters-in-law do not find such loving care from their mothers-in-law. Daughters-in-law are often treated as slaves in their marital home. Often the burden of work within the family falls on her shoulders and she is not fully accepted as part of the family but remains an outsider. Ruth seemed to forget about herself and focus on her mother-in-law. By taking her mind off herself and focusing on a particular task, she somehow got through this difficult period in her life.

Not only did Ruth cling to her mother-in-law, but also Naomi somehow made her God attractive to Ruth and Ruth committed herself to following Naomi's God. Unlike Jezebel, Ruth forsook her gods in favour of the one true God of Israel. She laid aside her lesser Moabite gods in exchange for the true God. She truly had found something better and discarded those former and now lesser gods that she used to worship.

Some people, though they turn to God, still stand in fear of other gods, so often they fail to let go of their traditional beliefs in case they incur the wrath of the gods. God demands our complete devotion and is not happy when we move back and forth in search of other gods.

Ruth left all behind. We need to do the same, to leave our gods behind and cleave to the One and Only true God, who is wholly trustworthy.

A determined woman of courage

"When Naomi realised that Ruth was determined to go with her, she stopped urging her." (Ruth 1:18)

Ruth could have made the choice to return to her homeland and family, to what was familiar and safe, but Ruth chose the more difficult option of going with Naomi to a strange land and people, not knowing what the future would hold, not knowing how the people known to be her nation's enemies would treat her. Ruth was a risk taker for God, facing a trip to an unknown destination and an unknown future.

Life is subject to change and sometimes it can change for the worse. Ruth found herself in difficult circumstances. Tragedy had entered into her life and decisions had to be made. Ruth's story is one of triumph over tragedy. Life can change for the worse, but it can also change for the better.

Ruth lost many things, but she never lost hope. In the midst of tragedy, we can lose our hope in God. Ruth never expected this tragedy in her life, but it came. At some point in all our lives, we will most likely face a tragedy or at least a difficult experience of one kind or another. So how can we handle tragedy and forge forward with hope?

Wisdom knows how to move forward in the face of calamity. As Ruth took steps to change things in her life, God was at work, turning a hopeless situation to one of victory. Ruth had many things against her. She was poor, a foreigner, a woman, and a childless widow. Ruth could have succumbed to living out her life as a victim of circumstances, but she chose to face the future positively. She did not lie down and bemoan her situation but got up to do something about it and her efforts were met with success. "Do not be overcome by evil but overcome evil with good." (Rom. 12:2)

A woman of initiative

> And Ruth the Moabitess said to Naomi, 'Let me go
> to the fields and pick up the leftover grain behind
> any in whose eyes I find favour.' Naomi said to her,
> 'Go ahead, my daughter.' So she went out and

> began to glean in the fields behind the harvesters.
> (Ruth 2:2-3)

Ruth was not content to sit and wallow in self-pity, but she actively made efforts to relieve her economic difficulties. She set about the task of gleaning. In the laws of Israel, this was one way that God had made provision for the destitute. "When you are harvesting in your field and you overlook a sheaf, do not go back to get it. Leave it for the alien, the fatherless and the widow." (Deut. 24:19) As Ruth took the first move to sort out her economic problems, God met that effort with kindness from Boaz. Boaz went the extra mile. He piled kindness on this poor destitute widow. He did more than was expected. Boaz is a good example for us to follow in going the extra mile to relieve others' physical hardships. Boaz took notice of her, though often in those days people overlooked foreigners and treated them with little respect.

> And her mother-in-law said to her, 'Where did you
> glean today? And where have you worked? Blessed
> be the man who took notice of you.' (Ruth 2:19)

Ruth did not know the ways in which her life would change from the apparent chance moment of entering the field of Boaz. Nevertheless, none of what happened to Ruth happened by chance, but God was in the background working out his good purpose and plan. God was at work behind the scenes, ordering events and orchestrating what appeared to be 'chance' meetings. *"What some call chance, luck or fate, the Hebrew Bible attributes to the sovereign hand of God."*[22]

A listener

> Naomi said to Ruth her daughter-in-law, 'It will be good for you, my daughter, to go with his girls, because in someone else's field you might be harmed.' So Ruth stayed close to her servant girls of Boaz to glean until the barley and wheat harvests were finished. (Ruth 2:22-23)

When advice was given, advice was taken. Ruth listened to what her mother-in-law, Naomi, suggested concerning how to attract Boaz's attention.

> 'Wash and perfume yourself and put on your best clothes. Then go down to the threshing floor, but don't let him know you are there until he has finished eating and drinking . . . He will tell you what to do.' (Ruth 3:3-4)

Not being familiar with the culture, Ruth needed Naomi's advice and was humble enough to receive it and follow it. "Listen to advice and accept instruction, and in the end you will be wise." (Prov. 19:20) Ruth was humble of heart and willing to listen to instruction and advice from someone older and wiser than she was. Ruth knew she could trust this old woman and knew she would not suggest something that would lead to her harm but would result in good for her. *Those who respect the elderly pave their own road to success."* (African Proverb)

A woman of good reputation

When Boaz noticed this foreign girl in his field, he showed her particular favour. When Ruth asked for the reason behind this special kindness he replied,

> 'I've been told all about what you have done for your mother-in-law since the death of your husband–how you left your father and mother and your homeland and came to live with a people you did not know before.' (Ruth 2:11)

Later when Ruth came to the threshing floor, Boaz again says " . . . All my fellow townsmen know that you are a woman of noble character." (Ruth 3:11) Ruth had earned for herself a good reputation. The people around her admired her qualities and spoke well of her. Ruth was better than 'seven sons.' (Ruth 4:15) In many societies, sons are often regarded to be of greater worth than daughters are, so Ruth is given a great tribute here. What a testimony!

A mother

> So Boaz took Ruth and she became his wife. Then he
> went to her, and the LORD enabled her to conceive,
> and she gave birth to a son. (Ruth 4:13)

Ruth had made difficult decisions, but now reaped the reward. The first part of her life was marred with childlessness and then finally by the tragic loss of her husband. Now, not only had God arranged for a husband for her, but she also had a son in whom she could delight.

Part of the lineage of Christ

"Salmon the father of Boaz, Boaz the father of Obed, Obed the father of Jesse, and Jesse the father of David." (Ruth 4:21-22)

The book of Ruth ends with this dramatic declaration of the fact that Ruth's own son was the ancestor of David. The most amazing part of this story is the way in which Ruth, a foreign woman from Moab becomes the great-grandmother of David, the king, and a member of the line of Christ.

> A record of the genealogy of Jesus Christ the son of David, the son of Abraham . . . Salmon the father of Boaz, whose mother was Rahab, Boaz the father of Obed, whose mother was Ruth, Obed the father of Jesse, and Jesse the father of King David. (Matt. 1:1-5)

Ruth was one of four women included in the genealogy of Jesus. God had truly turned things round for Ruth. For someone who appeared to have no future ahead of her, Ruth became a prominent person in Israel's history.

What lessons can we learn about God?

God is:

Sovereign over all the events of our lives

"Is it not from the mouth of the Most High that both calamities and good things come?" (Lam. 3:38) Sin has entered our world through man's disobedience and as a result, bad things happen in life. Life will not be perfect until we reach Heaven. For the believer, we know that "in all things, God works for the good of those who love him, who have been called according to his purpose." (Rom. 8:28) We can trust God in the face of trials, for his intentions are always good.

Not far from us

"Let your gentleness be evident to all. The Lord is near." (Phil. 4:5) God does not stand afar off but is close to us. He is intimately involved in our lives and is active on our behalf. He is kind towards us, generously providing us with all that we need. He may dwell on high, but also dwells with his people, for he is everywhere present.

Full of grace and help

"The LORD is with me; he is my helper." (Ps. 118:7) God meets with us in times of distress and crisis. He walks with us when we are in the valley of the shadow of death. God is the hope of the hopeless. He is the restorer of all our losses. In God's hands, what is lost can be found again.

We do not know our author's exact purpose. However, what is clear is that, through the insights we are given into rural life in twelfth and eleventh century B.C. Palestine; the everyday routines of life; the need to work; the joys of the family; the pains of bereavement; the parting from relatives; relationships with the mother-in-law, and from the illustration we are given of purity, innocence, faithfulness and loyalty, duty and love, the writer is wanting his readers to discern the hand of a God who cares, sustains and provides.[23]

Faithful to his people

> Blessed is he whose help is the God of Jacob, whose hope is the LORD his God, the Maker of heaven and earth, the sea and everything in them–the LORD, who remains faithful forever. (Ps. 146:5-6)

God does not run from us at the sight of danger. We can trust him, for he is faithful in both the good times and the bad. He will not disappoint. Man may fail us in times of trouble, but God is there for us.

The God of all nations

No nation can hold onto God as its exclusive right.

> Then Peter began to speak: 'I now realise how true it is that God does not show favouritism but accepts men from every nation who fear him and do what is right.' (Acts 10:34-35)

In Heaven, we will find men and women of every tribe, tongue, and nation. We need to reach out to those from other nations and give them the opportunity to hear and respond to the good news from God. Israel despised the Moabites, but God through the story of Ruth showed his acceptance of this Moabite who chose to follow him.

Kind

> And Naomi said to her daughter-in-law, 'May he be blessed by the LORD, whose kindness has not forsaken the living or the dead!' (Ruth 2:20)

God's kindness to us leads us to be kind to one another. Our human kindness one to another reflects the kindness of God.

Special Focus: Christ in the Story of Ruth

Apart from the already mentioned fact that Ruth was part of the lineage of Christ, there are ideas in Ruth's story that point forward to Christ. The image of Boaz, the kinsman-redeemer is an obvious one. A kinsman-redeemer is defined as a *"Male relative who, according to various laws found in the Pentateuch, had the privilege or responsibility to act for a relative who was in trouble, danger, or need of vindication."* [24] The main idea of the kinsman-redeemer was that of acting as a redeemer on behalf of a relative who was in need.

Jesus Christ is our kinsman-redeemer (our redeeming relative) who became one of us and rescued us in our need. (Heb. 2:11)

> In him we have redemption through his blood, the forgiveness of sins, in accordance with the riches of God's grace that he lavished on us with all wisdom and understanding. (Eph. 1:7-8)

Redemption contains the idea of being bought back. Boaz paid a price for the land so that he could redeem Ruth. Christ paid the price for our redemption on the cross. It cost Christ his life to redeem us, that is, to buy us back and to make us his very own. (See also 1 Cor. 6:20; 7:23)

Ruth herself is a portrait of self-sacrifice for Ruth gave up her own life for Naomi. "Greater love had no one than this that he lay down his life for his friends." (John 15:13) Christ is the perfect example of self-sacrifice. He gave up his glory to come to earth to become one of us so that he might act as our substitute. He then gave up his life and died on a cross so that our sins might be forgiven.

> You see at just the right time, when we were still powerless, Christ died for the ungodly. Very rarely will anyone die for a righteous man, though for a

good man someone might possibly dare to die. But God demonstrates his own love for us in this: While we were still sinners, Christ died for us. (Rom. 5:6-8)

For you know the grace of our Lord Jesus Christ, that though he was rich, yet for your sakes he became poor, so that you through his poverty might become rich. (2 Cor. 8:9)

For Further Discussion

1. Think about your own commitment to God. Have you entrusted your life to him, even as Ruth did?

2. Discuss Ruth's qualities as seen through Boaz' eyes.

3. "And we know that in all things God works for the good of those who love him, who have been called according to his purpose." (Rom. 8:28) Discuss this verse in light of life's 'ups and downs.'

Chapter Four
Abigail–A Woman who Prevented War

(Ref: 1 Sam. 25:1-44; 1 Sam. 27:3; 1 Sam. 30:3-5;

2 Sam. 2:2-3; 2 Sam. 3:3; 1 Chron. 3:1)

Name

Abigail means 'My father is Joy'[25] or 'Fountain of Joy.'[26]

Profile

- Married to a wealthy man named Nabal.

- Lived together with her husband at Carmel.

- Was a home manager and became known for her wisdom in securing peace.

Background

Abigail's story is intertwined with the story of David, a man after God's heart who had been anointed by Samuel as the next king of Israel. Saul, the king in office at the time, became his enemy and David was forced to move about from place to place. During this time, David travelled about with his army and often depended on the kindness of others to feed his men. The events concerning Nabal and Abigail took place sometime between 1020 and 1010 B.C.[27]

What lessons can we learn from Abigail's life?

Abigail was:

Married to a wealthy man

> A certain man in Maon, who had property there at Carmel, was very wealthy. He had a thousand goats and three thousand sheep, which he was shearing in Carmel. His name was Nabal and his wife's name was Abigail. (1 Sam. 25:2-3a)

Nabal is introduced as a very wealthy man. The extent of his wealth is emphasised by the record of his livestock. Nabal was a man of means with plenty to share with others, which is a great irony in light of what transpires next. Besides, it is also the time of shearing and resultant profit-making,[28] so Nabal has no excuse for any lack of generosity. *"Sheep-shearing was traditionally celebrated by feasting, with enough and to spare."*[29]

It is only at this point that his name is revealed, 'Nabal,' meaning 'fool,' and it comes as a surprise to the reader that this very wealthy man carries such an unfortunate name. As the story unfolds and Nabal makes some unwise decisions, the name will appear perfectly apt.

> For the fool speaks folly, his mind is busy with evil:
> He practices ungodliness and spreads error
> concerning the LORD; the hungry he leaves empty
> and from the thirsty he withholds water. (Is. 32:6)

The first mention of Abigail is that she is the wife to this very wealthy foolish man. Just as Nabal's wealth and folly is significant to the story, so also is the fact that Abigail is his wife, for she will turn out to be his saving grace.

A combination of wisdom and beauty

"She was an intelligent and beautiful woman, but her husband, a Calebite, was surly and mean in his dealings." (1 Sam. 23:3)

There is a deliberate contrast drawn here between the wife and the husband. Nabal is a 'fool' as his name suggests and also he is described as "harsh and badly behaved," (ESV) a further reflection of that folly. However,

Abigail is "discerning and beautiful." (ESV)

Abigail was a woman of 'good understanding,' demonstrating wisdom and discernment in her actions. Wisdom is not so much the possession of knowledge as it is a practical ability that we put to good use in our daily living. Abigail was gifted in applying such wisdom in her life.

Abigail was also gifted with beauty, no doubt both outward and inward. She was a beautiful and wise woman, a winning combination for Proverbs 11:22 states "Like a gold ring in a pig's snout is a beautiful woman who shows no discretion." Abigail's discernment and beauty will prove to be exactly what God uses to prevent a war from taking place. In contrast to Abigail, Nabal her husband, had neither beauty nor wisdom, and was the one responsible for almost bringing about the complete destruction of his family.

There seems to have been a big gap between Abigail and her husband. She is everything her husband is not. There is no doubt that Abigail, whether through her own personal choice or more likely through an arranged marriage, found herself married to a very difficult man. It certainly was not the ideal marriage but was a marriage of complete opposites with very little in common.

Despite the apparent mismatch and the trial of living with such a man, Abigail seems to fit well into the category of "a wife of noble character." (Prov. 31:10) Abigail sought Nabal's best and attempted to right his wrongs although he did not deserve it. She made up for her husband's foolishness by her wise actions. I wonder if Nabal ever realised the gem that he had in his wife. David certainly did and acknowledged the fact. David could see Abigail's excellence and when the opportunity presented itself, he made her his wife.

> Abigail's qualities, intelligence, and beauty, are precisely those of the man who the audience may already suspect will become her new husband . . . Abigail is as well matched with David as she is mismatched with Nabal.[30]

Approachable

> One of the servants told Nabal's wife Abigail: David sent messengers from the desert to give our master his greetings, but he hurled insults at them. Yet these men were very good to us. They did not mistreat us, and the whole time we were out in the fields near them noting was missing. Night and day they were a wall around us all the time we were

herding our sheep near them. Now think it over and see what you can do, because disaster is hanging over our master and his whole household. He is such a wicked man that no one can talk to him. (1 Sam. 25:14-17)

Again, another contrast is drawn between Abigail and Nabal. The servant reveals the detrimental situation that has arisen, to Abigail, while Nabal is "such a stubborn lout that no one can even talk to him." (1 Sam. 25:17 TLB) It would seem that the servant knew Abigail's character well. Perhaps this was not the first time that Abigail had stepped in to resolve the dilemmas created by her husband. Somehow, the servant knew she was a reasonable, astute woman, approachable and if the situation could be changed for good, she was the one to do it.

Abigail was unaware of what had happened between Nabal, and a delegation sent from David, and listens with intent to the servant's version of the events that had transpired in her absence.

No one could get through to Nabal and he certainly was not open to reason. "An unfriendly man pursues selfish ends; he defies all sound judgement." (Prov. 18:1) In contrast, Abigail was a listener and accepted the servant's account of events. The servant urged Abigail "Now think it over and see what you can do, because disaster is hanging over our master and his household." (1 Sam. 25:17)

Willing to take action

> Abigail lost no time. She took two hundred loaves of bread, two skins of wine, five dressed sheep, five seahs of roasted grain, a hundred cakes of raisins, two hundred cakes of pressed figs, and loaded them on donkeys. (1 Sam. 25:18)

Abigail *'lost no time'* for she realised the gravity of the situation. Abigail knew that she could not bury her head in the sand and hope that the problem went away. It needed wise handling and needed to be done quickly. She dealt swiftly with the escalating threat of war and David acknowledges this fact "if you had not come quickly." (1 Sam. 25:34)

Abigail handled her wealth wisely in contrast to Nabal who lacked generosity. Nabal's tight-fistedness and meanness of spirit had instigated this very situation, which threatened the existence of his family. Both his hands and his heart were closed towards David and his men. However, when God gives wealth, he expects us to be generous with it.

> Command those who are rich in this present world
> not to be arrogant nor to put their hope in wealth,
> which is so uncertain, but to put their hope in God,
> who richly provides us with everything for our
> enjoyment. Command them to do good, to be rich in
> good deeds, and to be generous and willing to
> share. In this way, they will lay up for themselves a
> firm foundation for the coming age, so that they
> may take hold of the life that is truly life. (1 Tim.
> 6:17-19)

Nabal forgot that what he possessed and treated as his own had come to him from God. *"All things come from God."* (James 1:17) Nabal took credit for all he had gained by his own hands and desired to hold on tightly to it declaring,

> Why should I take my bread and water, and the
> meat I have slaughtered for my shearers, and give it
> to men coming from who knows where? (1 Sam.
> 25:11)

In other words, he was not prepared to let others benefit from what he believed belonged to him. *"He is certainly not going to share his hard-won produce with the riffraff commanded by David."*[31]

Nabal reminds us of the man in the parable of the rich fool. (Luke 12:13-21) He built bigger barns to store all his grain and goods, not knowing that God would take his life that night and that he would never see all that he had set aside for himself to enjoy. In Nabal's case, he refused to share his abundant provisions with David and his men.

The irony lies in the fact that *"the provisions Nabal had refused will be provided by his more prudent and courteous wife."*[32] In order to resolve a threat to peace on her compound, Abigail wisely brought gifts to David and his men for "A gift opens the way for the giver and ushers him into the presence of the great." (Prov. 18:16)

Nabal made the mistake of forgetting to be rich toward God and his people.

> All the good that had been shown to Nabal's men on a previous occasion was completely negated by Nabal's insults. War was declared and his family now faced destruction.[33]

Abigail knew that the situation required urgent action, but also required the right approach. Gifts were needed to pave the way to peace and reconciliation.

Humble

> When Abigail saw David, she quickly got off her
> donkey and bowed down before David with her
> face to the ground. (1 Sam. 25:23)

Abigail's husband, Nabal was arrogant and proud. When David's men approached Nabal peaceably and graciously requesting assistance, Nabal responded rudely, "Who is this David? Who is this son of Jesse? Many servants are breaking away from their masters these days" (v.10) In other words, Nabal, in front of David's men, demonstrated his contempt for David. In his own eyes, Nabal was a 'big man' while David was a 'small boy.' David's men came in peace but were rewarded with insult. Nabal did not merely refuse the request but treated the request with absolute disdain. *"Nabal, in rather less than polite terms, tells them to get lost!"*[34]

However, Abigail was noticeably different. She was a woman of humility and grace. Abigail showed respect and honour toward David. Throughout her interaction with him, she demonstrated, in both action and speech, a deep humility and the fact that she held David in high esteem. Her conversation is characterised throughout by the word 'lord' when referring to David and the word 'servant' when making reference to her. Even later in the story Abigail shows a willingness to demonstrate such humility in action. "Behold your handmaid is a servant to wash the feet of the servants of my lord." (1 Sam. 25:41) Abigail was a truly a woman of humility.

Willing to take responsibility

> She fell at his feet and said: 'My lord, let the blame be on me alone. Please let your servant speak to you; hear what your servant has to say. (1 Sam. 25:24)

> Please forgive your servant's offense . . . (1 Sam. 25:28a)

Abigail is quick to apologise for how David was treated in her household, even though she is not the actual person who caused the grievance. Though Abigail was not around when David's men made the request for provisions, Abigail takes full responsibility for what has happened in her absence. She makes it clear that had she been there, things would not have transpired as they did. While taking responsibility, she urges David to disregard the treatment meted out by her unwise husband.

Our speech can either destroy or build up. "He who

loves a pure heart and whose speech is gracious will have the king for his friend." (Prov. 22:11) It is a pity that Nabal did not know this. David, as the future king could have been a very helpful friend to him. "A man of knowledge uses words with restraint, and a man of understanding is even-tempered." (Prov. 17:27) Nabal was neither a man of knowledge nor understanding. In contrast, Abigail was careful when she approached David. She quickly says *'Don't be offended'* and acknowledges the wrong done to David and his men. *"David's anger may have been assuaged by the smell of food, but Abigail's very skilful and accomplished speech completely won him over."* [35] In taking responsibility and using carefully thought-through words, Abigail defuses the tense situation. "Pleasant words are a honeycomb, sweet to the soul and healing to the bones." (Prov. 16:24)

We need to be careful about what we say and how we say it. We are told in Matthew 12:36 "But I tell you that men will have to give account on the day of judgement for every careless word they have spoken." and in Colossians 4:6 "Let your conversation be always full of grace, seasoned with salt, so that you may know how to answer everyone."

Nabal's harsh words were met with words of war from

David. "Put on your swords!" (1 Sam. 25:13) Proverbs 15:1 states, "A gentle answer turns away wrath, but a harsh word stirs up dissension." While Nabal's words set a war in motion, Abigail's words worked to avert the disaster. Our speech brings with it consequences, so we need to be careful to use our tongues to promote good and not evil.

A woman who knew when to speak and when not to speak

"But she did not tell her husband." (1 Sam. 25:19)

> " . . . he was in high spirits and very drunk. So she told him nothing until daybreak. Then in the morning, when Nabal was sober, his wife told him all these things . . ." (1 Sam. 25:36-37)

Abigail knew not only what to say, but also when to speak. There were times when it was wise to keep things quiet and times to reveal them. In the first case above, it was wise to act to divert danger, rather than give her husband the opportunity to stand in the way of peace. In the second case, her husband was in an unfit state to talk to, being "in high spirits and very drunk."

That same gift of timing came into play when Abigail

spoke to David. While she decides, for the moment, not to speak to her husband, she knows that it is vital to begin immediate negotiations with David. He is an angry man and needs to be persuaded to change his mind before it is too late. Thankfully, her words pleased David.

Willing to be used by God

"David said to Abigail, 'Praise be to the LORD, the God of Israel, who has sent you today to meet me.'" (1 Sam. 25:35)

> Abigail's actions are the proximate cause for David's escaping guilt, but the real protector of the future king's integrity is Yahweh himself.[36]

In other incidences when David had opportunity to take revenge on his enemy Saul, David seemed to have the inner strength to avoid bloodshed, but in this particular situation with Nabal, Abigail is God's particular instrument in helping David to avoid *"the temptation to violence that comes with power."*[37]

David acknowledged the fact that he had been tempted to take matters into his own hands here but for the intervention of God through this godly woman. Such action would have been detrimental to his future. " . . . man's anger does not bring about the righteous life that God desires." (James 1:20)

The rejected king may practise sheer butchery but that is not the way for the chosen king. Yet the chosen one wanted his gore and would have obtained it had Yahweh not sent him a saviour in skirts.[38]

A woman of good judgement

May you be blessed for your good judgement and for keeping me from bloodshed this day and from avenging myself with my own hands. (1 Sam. 25:33)

Abigail was very astute and had evaluated the threat that faced her family. She had judged the situation accurately and had handled it well. Meanwhile, at home Nabal was holding "a banquet like that of a king." (1 Sam. 25:36) Nabal was totally unaware of the trouble his folly had stirred up. He was celebrating when it would have been more appropriate to fast. Nabal seemed oblivious to the fact that Abigail was away trying to clean up his mess. Abigail was an insightful woman, seeing ahead the repercussions of her husband's folly and the problems that David the future king would bring into his own life, if he took matters into his own hands.

A peacemaker

> Then David accepted from her hand what she had
> brought him and said, 'Go home in peace. I have
> heard your words and granted your request. (1 Sam.
> 25:35)

Abigail became the peacemaker in this situation. "Blessed are the peacemakers for they will be called children of God." (Matt. 5:9) Peacemakers reflect their Heavenly Father's character. Some women urge others to respond in violence toward supposed threats, for example, Zeresh, Haman's wife.

> His wife Zeresh and all his friends said to him,
> 'Have a gallows built, seventy five feet high and ask
> the king in the morning to have Mordecai hanged
> on it.' (Est. 5:14)

Such foolish advice brought about the death of her own husband for he was hung on the very gallows intended for Mordecai. Instead, we are encouraged to "Make every effort to live in peace with all men and to be holy; without holiness no one will see the Lord." (Heb. 12:14) "If it is possible, as far as it depends on you, live at peace with everyone." (Rom. 12:18)

By her swift intervention, Abigail prevented a disaster from happening. It is not an easy task to stand in the middle between two opposing forces. Sometimes when disagreements occur, we have to try to help people to see the situation from different perspectives. We also need to know when to intervene in a problem and when it is wise to stand back. Not all conflicts are ours to resolve. "Like one who seizes a dog by the ears, is a passer-by who meddles in a quarrel not his own." (Prov. 26:17) Nevertheless, Abigail knew that this was her problem and knew what she had to do. "Do not be overcome with evil but overcome evil with good." (Rom. 12:21) Those who have made their peace with God are required to make their peace with others. It is not easy to be a mediator, but it is important to be one.

Many tribal, village and religious clashes are preventable if women played the role of peacemakers. "There is deceit in the hearts of those who plot evil, but joy for those who promote peace." (Prov. 12:20) How our society needs peacemakers! In times of crisis, women of courage can step in to prevent disaster. Women need to become agents of peace. This is something that requires much effort and hard work.

As far as it is within our power, we are to work towards peace. Long-standing rivalries may take time to resolve, but we must not lose heart, but keep trying to see warring communities reconciled. Abigail shows us that it can be achieved. In the face of David's anger and vow to destroy all the males in Nabal's household, Abigail, a woman is the ideal intercessor.[39] A man in that situation might not have been given a hearing. *"It is easy to see in Abigail how a woman's gifts may effectively be used in negotiation and in defusing a dangerous situation."*[40]

"' . . . I have heard your words and granted your request.'" (1 Sam. 25:35) David's change of heart and subsequent response alleviated Abigail's concern for her household and Abigail was able to breathe a sigh of relief knowing that the danger had been averted. She was an effective counsellor and negotiator who worked hard to prevent Nabal (her present husband) and David (her future husband) from making rash moves. Here God saves David *"from himself, or rather from the consequences of deeds potentially disastrous to his own interests."*[41]

A woman of courage and an overcomer

Abigail found herself in a difficult marriage, but she was victorious over her circumstances. Abigail, no doubt, faced many trials while married to Nabal. However, if this instance is anything to go by, she handled them well. Normally in life, "Bad company corrupts good character," (1 Cor. 15:33) yet Abigail had managed to retain her gracious character as she lived in company with a difficult man.

Abigail risked her life when she faced David and his men with swords raised ready for battle. However, her courageous actions saved her entire family from destruction. We might ask ourselves 'What can one woman do?' Abigail's example demonstrates that one woman can do a lot, with God on her side.

What lessons can we learn about God?

God is:

A peacemaker who uses his servants to prevent disaster

> Let us therefore make every effort to do what leads to peace and to mutual edification. Do not destroy the work of God for the sake of food. (Rom. 14:19-20)

"Blessed are the peacemakers." (Matt. 5:9) Despite the risk to her own life, Abigail moved swiftly into action to forge a pathway of peace. She spoke graciously to the offended party and brought gifts with her and in doing so Abigail averted a disaster of untold proportion. *"David recognised the God-given wisdom of her words, and never regretted acting on her advice."*[42]

A God who restrains his people from evil

> May you be blessed for your good judgement and for keeping me from bloodshed this day and from avenging myself with my own hands. Otherwise as surely as the LORD, the God of Israel, lives, who has kept me from harming you, if you had not come quickly to meet me, not one male belonging to Nabal would have been left by daybreak. (1 Sam. 25:33-34)

God, through his obedient servant acted to prevent David from committing bloodshed.

> It was a major lesson in David's training for kingship, and one that he was going to need to keep before him at future crises. The implication is that violence breeds violence, whereas restraint makes way for a peaceful solution.[43]

God can intervene and give us grace to refrain from evil.

An avenger of evil

"About ten days later, the Lord struck Nabal, and he died." (1 Sam. 25:38)

> When David heard that Nabal was dead, he said, 'Praise be to the LORD, who has upheld my cause against Nabal for treating me with contempt. He has kept his servant from doing wrong and has brought Nabal's wrongdoing down on his own head. (1 Sam. 25:39)

Nabal was a king in his own eyes, while he failed to receive God's chosen future king with honour. God did not treat this insult lightly for in slighting God's servant, Nabal had slighted God. Abigail restrained David from taking revenge, allowing God room to act on David's behalf.

David had a right to be angry, for Nabal had paid him back evil for good (1 Sam. 26:21), but the prerogative for revenge lay with God.

> Do not take revenge, my friends, but leave room for God's wrath, for it is written: 'It is mine to avenge; I will repay, says the Lord.' (Rom. 12: 19)

What David might have used his troops to do, God did ten days later. If he had taken matters into his own hands, he would have had to deal with the guilt of his actions and would have missed seeing God in action. We do not need to respond rashly to our enemy's insults but need to leave the matter in God's hands. God can handle things for us!

A provider of peace

"When a man's ways are pleasing to the LORD, he makes even his enemies live at peace with him." (Prov. 16:7) The Hebrew word 'shalom' means more than peace, but wholeness and completeness. It contains the idea of good relationships with others and fulfilment in one's undertakings.[44] The equivalent Greek word, *'eirene,'* suggests *'a situation which results from the cessation of hostilities or war'* and can also mean *'peaceful conduct towards others.'* It also implies the idea of a peace that prevails internally even in the midst of external conflict.[45] Someone once said, *"Peace is not the absence of conflict, but the presence of God no matter what the conflict."*

Special Focus: Christ in the Story of Abigail

In the Old Testament Isaiah prophesied that Jesus would be called the Prince of Peace.

> For to us a child is born, to us a son is given, and the government will be on his shoulders. And he will be called Wonderful Counsellor, Mighty God, Everlasting Father, Prince of Peace. (Isa. 9:6)

Jesus is the Great Reconciler, and he has given his followers the ministry of reconciliation. 2 Cor. 5:18-19 assures us that,

> All this is from God, who reconciled us to himself through Christ and gave us the ministry of reconciliation; that God was reconciling the world to himself in Christ, not counting men's sins against them. And he has committed to us the message of reconciliation.

Since the fall of man, people have been separated from God because of sin. Christ by his death on the cross has restored our peace with God and with each other. As

Christians, we are urged not just to live at peace with each other but to seek peace and pursue it. (See Heb. 12:13; 1 Pet. 3:11) God has given us the task of reconciliation.

This task lies at the heart of the Gospel, for in all Christian involvement in transforming conflict an invitation to escape from the deepest of all alienations by being reconciled to God through Christ is implicitly enshrined. The root cause of all conflict is a life out of kilter with the loving purposes of God. So, the only hope for a lasting peace between individuals and peoples is to be at peace with God through Jesus Christ.[46]

Abigail acts as the saviour of both her husband Nabal and the future king, David. Jesus is the Saviour of the World who saves us from our sins. "Salvation is found in no one else, for there is no other name under heaven given to men by which we must be saved." (Acts 4:12)

For Further Discussion

1. Faced with Abigail's situation (both in her daily marriage to a difficult man and in the immediate situation of approaching calamity) how do you think you might have reacted? What do you think enabled Abigail to act with such courage and wisdom?

2. In Philippians 4:2 Paul urges a fellow companion to intervene to help Euodia and Syntyche to reconcile their differences. Mediation in such disputes requires wisdom. What are the practical steps that you could take to mediate between two people caught up in a dispute?

3. Christ has destroyed the dividing wall between us and God, and us and each other. How can we put that truth into practice in our communities where we live side by side with people of different tribes and races?

Chapter Five
Jezebel - A Woman Who Had Other Gods

(Ref: 1 Kings 16:30- 31; 1 Kings 18:4; 1 Kings 19:1-2;

1 Kings 21:1-29; 2 Kings 9:30-37)

Name

Jezebel means *'Where is the prince? The prince is Baal.'*[47] In the winter months, people chanted this phrase to usher in the spring of the year. Certainly, Jezebel was a devotee of Baal.[48] It may also mean *'unexalted or unhusbanded.'*[49]

Profile

- Daughter of Ethbaal, King of the Sidonians.

- A queen married to King Ahab.

- A mother.

Background

Jezebel's story takes place during the time of the Divided

Kingdom: Israel in the North and Judah in the South. This was a time marred both by different dynasties struggling with each other to gain and hold unto political power, and by fighting between Israel and Judah. During this particular period Israel was also battling against the powerful nation of Assyria, to which it succumbed finally in 721 B.C. Ahab, Jezebel's husband became king in 874 B.C.[50]

What lessons can we learn from Jezebel's life?

Jezebel was:

Married to Ahab

> Ahab son of Omri did more evil in the eyes of the LORD than any of those before him. He not only considered it trivial to commit the sins of Jeroboam, son of Nebat, but he also married Jezebel, daughter of Ethbaal, king of the Sidonians, and began to serve Baal and worship him. (1 Kings 16: 30-31)

Omri, Ahab's father had reigned for twelve years over Northern Israel. Possibly, for the purpose of protection against threatening powers from the east, Omri made an alliance with the Phoenicians through the marriage of his son Ahab to Jezebel. Politically it may have appeared the right move, but for Israel's spiritual life, it proved disastrous.

> But Omri did evil in the eyes of the LORD and sinned more than all those before him. He walked in all the ways of Jeroboam, son of Nebat and in his sin, which he had caused Israel to commit, so that they provoked the LORD, the God of Israel, to anger by their worthless idols. (1 Kings 16: 25-26)

Ahab appears to have followed his father's example. It is interesting to note that his name means *'brother of the father.'*[51] Apparently, he followed his father in his evil ways and even went far beyond his father's evil example.

> He set up an altar for Baal that he built in Samaria. Ahab also made an Asherah pole and did more to provoke the LORD, the God of Israel, to anger than did all the kings of Israel before him. (1 Kings 16:32-33)

Unfortunately, Ahab was a weak husband, somehow unable to stand up to his wife and prevent his wife from carrying out her evil plans. He was a man with little or no faith in God, and therefore, he was easily swayed. He stood back and had little influence in his wife's life. It is not always good for a man to allow a wife to continue to do what she wants to do, especially if she is walking contrary to God's ways. Ahab seems to have had little respect for God, as he readily gives up on God in favour of the gods his wife worshipped. *"He could not restrain her and instead joined her in having a temple built for Baal in Samaria."*[52]

An influence for evil

> There was never a man like Ahab, who sold himself
> to do evil in the eyes of the LORD, urged on by
> Jezebel his wife. (1 Kings 21: 25)

Jezebel was the driving force behind her husband's choice of living an evil life. She urged him on, rather than restraining him from evil. She was totally opposite to a woman like Abigail. (See Chapter Four: Abigail) Women hold a huge power of influence over their husbands and over their families. Women, therefore, can be a huge influence for good and, unfortunately, for bad in their families' lives.

Godly spouses are to urge their partners on to good works. God's word points out that "Bad company corrupts good character." (1 Cor. 15:33) We need to be careful of the kind of company we keep, and particularly of the kind of person we choose to spend the rest of our lives with. Jezebel not only influenced her husband but also was determined to make all Israel worship her gods. She was intent on wiping out the worship of God in Israel. As a result, she met a bitter end and was thrown down from her high position.

What a legacy to be known as a wife who urged her husband on to do evil! Jezebel is renowned as the most evil woman in the Bible and a model of those who reject God.

A foreign idol worshipper

Just like Jezebel, Ruth was a foreigner, but Ruth was different because she wisely decided to worship the true God. (See Chapter Three: Ruth) In contrast, Jezebel brought her gods with her and clung to them tightly. Jezebel particularly worshipped Baal, the chief Canaanite *'storm and fertility deity,'*[53] who was often worshipped by means of child sacrifice. In addition, sexual rituals played a major part in his worship. Such practices were abominable to God and, because of the continuation of the worship of Baal amongst Israel, God allowed the land to be afflicted by drought. Queen Jezebel influenced the people of Israel, and they failed to maintain their covenant relationship with God. Their unfaithfulness led them into punishment.

"Whoever sacrifices to any god, other than the LORD alone, shall be devoted to destruction." (Ex. 22:20) We need to be careful whom we follow!

Some women hold unto idols and continue to wield strong influence over their families and communities. Many who attend Christian churches also continue to hold onto their family gods and ancestral traditions, as a precaution 'just in case.' However, God demands exclusive worship. He is a jealous God.

> You shall not make for yourself an idol in the form of anything in heaven above or on the earth beneath or in the waters below. You shall not bow down to them or worship them; for I the LORD your God am a jealous God. (Ex. 20:4-6)

> Joshua said to the people, 'You are not able to serve the LORD. He is a holy God; he is a jealous God. He will not forgive your rebellion and your sins. If you forsake the LORD and serve foreign gods, he will turn and bring disaster on you and make an end of you, after he has been good to you.' (Josh. 24:19-20)

A persecutor of God's prophets

> While Jezebel was killing off the LORD's prophets, Obadiah had taken a hundred prophets and hidden them in two caves . . . (1 Kings 18:4)

Jezebel had no fear of God and as a result had no fear of killing his prophets or messengers. What foolishness to choose to stand against God and to be unafraid to pick a fight with his servants!

When Jezebel became queen, she had surrounded herself with her own prophets who spoke only what she wanted to hear. Such people still exist today, even in the Church. Paul warns Timothy, a young minister about a time when,

> . . . men will not put up with sound doctrine. Instead, to suit their own desires, they will gather around them a great number of teachers to say what their itching ears want to hear. (2 Tim. 4:3)

One particular prophet called Elijah was a problem for Jezebel. She could exercise control over her own prophets, but not over Elijah. In contrast to her husband, Elijah was a man of deep conviction and faith in God. He was not prepared to allow this woman, regardless of her high position as queen and despite the personal consequences, to continue in her wicked ways, turning the hearts of the people of Israel away from God. Jezebel did not want to hear the truth which Elijah the true prophet of God spoke.

Elijah, to her, was a thorn in the flesh that needed plucking out, and quickly. As far as Jezebel was concerned Elijah had gone one step too far when he killed her precious prophets. Jezebel was furious and declared war on Elijah.

> May the gods deal with me, be it ever so severely, if
> by this time tomorrow I do not make your life like
> that of one of them. (1 Kings 19:1-2)

Jezebel as queen, enjoyed doing as she pleased, and Elijah stood in the way of her freedom to do anything she wanted, when she wanted. So Jezebel was prepared to stop at nothing to get him out of her way. The only life that mattered to her was her own. Elijah meant nothing to her. This prophet of God was standing in her way and she was prepared to wipe him out. Jezebel showed no restraint.

Despite her threats and real attempts to rid herself of this annoying and inconvenient prophet, Jezebel did not succeed. Jezebel's threats of murder fell to the ground. God gave Jezebel every opportunity to change from her wicked ways, by sending his messenger to her, but she refused to heed the word of God.

Manipulative

> Jezebel his wife said, 'Is this how you act as king over Israel? Get up and eat! Cheer up. I'll get you the vineyard of Naboth the Jezreelite.' (1 Kings 21:7)

The story of Naboth's vineyard shows Jezebel in a very poor light. Much to the queen's surprise, the king was depressed when Naboth refused to sell his field to him. Jezebel could not understand her husband's weakness as king, so she decided to take over the matter. No mere human being was going to stand in the way of the king getting what he wanted.

In order to get what she wanted; Jezebel set her wicked plan in motion. She would stop at nothing to get the vineyard. She bent the law to suit her own ends and arranged for the death of Naboth. (See 1 Kings 21: 1-16). Sad to say, even today people bribe members of the legal profession in an effort to pervert justice. Others arrange for the assassination of those who stand in their way of getting what they want. God would say,

> Do not pervert justice or show partiality. Do not accept a bribe, for a bribe blinds the eyes of the wise and twists the words of the righteous. Follow justice

and justice alone, so that you may live and possess
the land the LORD your God is giving you. (Deut.
16:19-20)

Jezebel is an example of how power corrupts. She believed that being in authority meant one could behave anyhow. *"Jezebel took a deceitful and violent approach to solving the problem."*[54] Rules and laws were for others to obey, but not for her. Jezebel felt no remorse for her abuse of power, but Jezebel did face consequences for her actions. She may have achieved her purpose and got what she wanted but, in the end, what seemed so pleasing to the eye ended up becoming a burial plot for her son. She became a cold-blooded murderer, all for the sake of a field. Jezebel was a too-devoted wife, who was prepared to stop at nothing to help maintain her husband's authority as king.

It is not always good to get what you want. Because of Jezebel's murderous plot, Elijah declared many penalties to Ahab. Among them, the promise that dogs would "devour Jezebel by the wall of Jezreel." (1 Kings 21:23) As prophesied by Elijah, Jezebel died in this disgraceful manner, Jezebel's husband died in battle, while Jehu killed her son. Jezebel wanted power for herself, her husband, and her son, but in the end, she did not live to enjoy it. It is good to remember, *"Only one life, twill soon be past, only what's done for Christ will last."* (C.T. Studd) We all have one chance at life, and it is good to remember our Creator in the days of our youth. (Eccles. 12:1)

Ahab was not without blame in this evil plan. In standing back and allowing Jezebel to secure Naboth's vineyard by devious means, Ahab was turning his back on God's laws. "Do not defraud your neighbour or rob him." (Lev. 19:13) Ahab had no right to Naboth's land. He should have told his wife this, instead of sulking over the fact that Naboth had refused to give up what rightfully belonged to him. Therefore, his wife's actions also brought repercussions into his own life. Jezebel's husband refused to take up his responsibility to lead but passed it over to his wife. Unfortunately, Jezebel's choices became a source of death to him. The king had denied his responsibility to uphold justice and as a result had to face severe consequences. "By justice, a king gives a country stability, but one who is greedy for bribes tears it down." (Prov. 29:4)

A woman of commitment

Jezebel was committed to herself, her husband, and her gods. Where our commitment lies, is important. If Jezebel's commitment had been toward God first, it might have become a trait of virtue in her life. Unfortunately, in Jezebel's case it was used for evil purposes, for she was committed to pursuing her own interests. In contrast, Christians ought not to pursue their own interests, but the interests of others. (Phil. 2:21)

Devoid of wisdom

"The fear of the LORD is the beginning of knowledge, but fools despise wisdom and discipline." (Prov.1: 7)

Jezebel and her husband Ahab lacked wisdom, demonstrated by the fact that they followed other gods and abandoned the worship of the one true God for the sake of political advantage and earthly treasures. Jezebel followed the wrong gods. Her courage, abilities, and strength of will, might have been put to positive use in the hands of the true God. She made wrong choices and, unfortunately, influenced others to make further wrong choices and to worship false gods.

Jezebel had no thought for tomorrow. She forgot that one day she would reap a reward for the life she lived. Jezebel died a terrible death and her life amounted to nothing. All she left behind was a legacy of sin. In her death, she faced the ultimate humiliation. A lack of a proper burial is a thing of disgrace, even today. Nevertheless, this was the outcome of Jezebel's wicked ways, her disastrous influence, and evil policies. Ahab and his wife Jezebel challenged God and lost the battle.

We remember Jezebel because of her life of evil and not for any good that she did. She committed crimes against God's people and corrupted Israel's faith in the one and only God.

Involved in witchcraft

> 'How can there be peace,' Jehu replied, 'as long as all the idolatry and witchcraft of your mother Jezebel abound?' (2 Kings 9:22)

Jezebel appears to have been involved in witchcraft and left a legacy that continued long after she died. Some men and women are actively involved in witchcraft or sorcery.

They charge fees from vulnerable people who go to them seeking assistance in the form of a spell or a curse.

God states clearly in his word,

I will set my face against the person who turns to mediums and spiritists to prostitute himself by following them, and I will cut them off from his people. (Lev. 20:6)

Involvement in witchcraft and related activities is detestable to God.

Let no one be found among you who sacrifices his son or daughter in the fire, who practices divination or sorcery, interprets omens, engages in witchcraft, or casts spells, or who is a medium or spiritist or who consults the dead. Anyone who does these things is detestable to the LORD, and because of these detestable practices the LORD your God will drive those nations before you. You must be blameless before the LORD your God. (Deut. 18:10-25)

God denounced Manasseh, one of the kings of Judah, for his involvement in such practices.

And he did what was evil in the sight of the LORD, according to the despicable practices of the nations whom the LORD drove out before the people of

> Israel. . . . And he burnt his son as an offering and used fortune telling and omens and dealt with mediums and with necromancers. He did much evil in the sight of the LORD, provoking him to anger. (2 Kings 21:2-6 ESV)

In the time of Moses, God gave the people prophets so that they would not look to sorcerers or diviners.

> The nations you will dispossess listen to those who practise sorcery or divination. But as for you, the LORD your God has not permitted you to do so. The LORD your God will raise up for you a prophet like me from among your own brothers. You must listen to him. (Deut. 18:14-15)

As Christians today we have God's word, which is a lamp to our feet and a light for our path. (Ps. 119:105) In His word, God has revealed to us his mind, his heart, and his will for humankind. In it, we will find the wisdom needed to walk daily with our God. We also have the Holy Spirit as our teacher who guides us into all truth.

There is a lot of fear surrounding witchcraft that can be paralysing and can even cause mental and physical illnesses. The Bible acknowledges the power of evil, but Christians know that God's power is greater. Therefore, as women of God we need to rise up with faith and courage in the face of evil, for God's power can overcome evil. Know that "the one who is in you is greater than the one who is in the world." (1 John 4:4) Jesus has given his servants authority over demons. (See also Mark 16:17-18)

There is a growing problem of accusations of involvement in witchcraft especially in some African societies. Many of these accusations are false, leading to innocent victims suffering terribly. Some victims have had nails driven through their skulls while others have been hung upside down. More have been poisoned, drowned, buried alive and burnt alive.[55] To their shame, some pastors have been involved in pointing the finger at individuals, often children, and are guilty of inciting others to administer torture to some of these innocent victims. Mothers of Africa, rise up to protect these vulnerable ones.

What lessons can we learn about God?

God is:

A jealous God

"For the Lord your God is a consuming fire, a jealous God." (Deut. 4:24) God alone is worthy of worship and he will not tolerate any rivals. We need to protect our hearts and ensure that nothing else takes first place in our hearts, for that place is reserved for God alone.

In control

"Though they plot evil against you and devise wicked schemes they cannot succeed." (Ps. 21:11) At times, it seems like the wicked prosper and have the upper hand, but God thwarts the plans of the wicked. He knows all things and no secrets are hidden from him.

Gracious and merciful

God does not easily give up on people but sends his messengers to them repeatedly. Jezebel had every opportunity to turn from her wickedness, but she failed to do so. "Those who cling to worthless idols forfeit the grace that could be theirs." (Jonah 2:8 cf. 2 Kings 17:15) In holding on to what she believed was important, she failed to take hold of the most precious thing that is, faith in the true and living God.

Special Focus: Christ in the Story of Jezebel

Though very seldom pointed out, Jezebel is part of the ancestry of Christ as her daughter Athaliah married Jehoram, who is included as part of Jesus' ancestry in

Matthew's account. "Asa the father of Jehoshaphat, Jehoshaphat the father of Jehoram, Jehoram the father of Uzziah." (Matt. 1:8)

Jezebel is a picture of a life lived without God. Christ died to save us from our sins. We can choose to trust Christ and be saved or to live without God and suffer the consequences.

This wicked queen went to great lengths to destroy her enemies. This contrasts greatly with Jesus who died for his enemies that they might be saved.

For Further Discussion

1. What is the danger of having one foot in a church and one in secret societies or in witchcraft?

2. Jezebel left behind her a legacy of evil and her life influenced many after to follow her evil ways. Think about what kind of legacy you would like to leave behind.

3. Compare and contrast Jezebel and Esther who similarly played the role of 'a queen.' What made the difference between them?

Chapter Six
Esther - A Woman Who Saved her People.

(Ref: Esther Chaps. 1-9)

Name

Esther (her Persian name) means star, which could express the idea of Esther's radiance or beauty; Hadassah (her Hebrew name) means 'myrtle,' which was a small tree known for its delicate fragrance.[56]

Profile

- A Jew.

- An orphan raised by her cousin, Mordecai.

- A lady of great beauty, brought to the palace, where she found the favour of the king and was made queen, the wife to King Ahasuerus or Xerxes.

Background

Esther's story takes place in the Persian Empire. Years earlier God's people had been captured and brought to live here. Esther became queen in 479 B.C.[57]

What lessons can we learn from Esther's life?

Esther was:

An orphan

> Mordecai had a cousin named Hadassah, whom he had brought up because she had neither father nor mother. . . . and Mordecai had taken her as his own daughter when her father and mother died. (Est. 2:7)

Esther at an early age lost both parents. This tragedy could have placed Esther in an extremely vulnerable situation with an insecure and loveless future, but Esther was fortunate that Mordecai, a family member, stepped in to take up the responsibility to raise her.

Mordecai took her as his own daughter, and it is clear throughout the story of Esther that he cared for her and that she respected and loved him even as her own father. When Esther was taken to the king's palace, it is recorded,

> Every day he (Mordecai) walked back and forth
> near the courtyard of the harem to find out how
> Esther was and what was happening to her. (Est.
> 2:11)

Later when the plot against the Jews had been exposed and Mordecai came in mourning clothes to the gate of the palace, Esther was concerned. "When Esther's maids and eunuchs came and told her about Mordecai, she was in great distress." (Est. 4:4a) Mordecai undoubtedly knew that taking on an orphan would be a big task, but he did what was right and because of his love for and care of this vulnerable orphan, he had gained a precious daughter and had established a loving relationship that would continue throughout his lifetime. The gains had far outweighed the inconvenience of another mouth to feed.

Many children in Africa face the threat of becoming orphans due to religious conflicts, fatal accidents, and the problem of HIV/AIDS.[58] Orphans face many challenges in life such as emotional trauma, separation from siblings, lack of support, exploitation and abuse, poverty and stigma, particularly if the parent dies of AIDS. God is concerned for these vulnerable ones, and we need to reach out a helping hand to them in their predicament, so that they like Esther might have a hope and a future.

Mordecai devotedly looked out for Esther's welfare. Sadly, when some extended family members take an orphaned child into their home, they often treat them as slaves and as a burden to their family. Ill-treatment is the lot of many an orphan adding to the trauma of losing their parents. *"It is only when the soup sours that an orphan gets an unusually large amount."* (Nigerian Proverb) Life is tough for the orphan, though it need not be.

There was no evidence that Esther felt bitter because she lost her parents. The solution for Esther's problem was God's provision of a loving and compassionate cousin, who selflessly devoted himself to Esther's care. One of the solutions for the problem of increasing numbers of orphans is adoption. There are couples who for various reasons have not been able to have children of their own. Many would love to adopt needy orphans to take the place of the children they are not able to have. Not only has Mordecai set us an example to follow, but also an even greater example comes from God himself. God has graciously adopted us and lavished his love on us.

> In love he (God) predestined us to be adopted as his sons through Jesus Christ, in accordance with his pleasure and will. (Eph. 1:4-5)

God is concerned about orphans and is in favour of adoption. We need to work to eradicate the stigma that surrounds orphans themselves as well as the stigma surrounding adoption. Orphans need to be taken under our wings and loved as our own children.

A Jew

Esther's family were amongst the Jews taken into captivity by King Nebuchadnezzar. When King Cyrus permitted the Jews to return to their homeland, Esther's parents had chosen to stay in Persia. Mordecai, Esther's guardian was a Jew and Esther was raised as a member of the Jewish community, a minority people under the control of a foreign pagan Persian government.

When Esther was taken to the palace, Mordecai's advice to Esther was to keep her nationality and family background quiet.

> Esther had not revealed her nationality and family
> background, because Mordecai had forbidden her to
> do so. (Est. 2:10)

"But Esther had kept secret her family background and nationality just as Mordecai had told her to do . . ." (Est. 2:20) It appears that Mordecai knew that there was a time and a place to reveal such things. Esther's nationality would become significant in due course and would need to be revealed, but for now, Esther was to keep it to herself. Both her Jewish background and her new position would place Esther in the influential position of acting as her people's intermediary.

Beautiful and winsome

" . . . This girl, who was also known as Esther was lovely in form and features . . ." (Est. 2:7)

God had bestowed remarkable beauty upon Esther. This gift, in turn was used by God to place Esther in the right place at the right time for the rescue of God's people.

> Now the king was attracted to Esther more than to
> any of the other women, and she won his favour
> and approval more than any of the other virgins. So
> he set a royal crown on her head and made her
> queen instead of Vashti. (Est. 2:17)

Esther's beauty demonstrates that God gives the gift of beauty, and it can be used for his glory and purpose.

Humble

" . . . she continued to follow Mordecai's instructions as she had done when he was bringing her up." (Est. 2:20)

Esther had grown up to respect Mordecai and to heed his advice. Not only that, but when taken to the king's palace Esther was happy to be advised by Hegai, the man set in charge of the king's wives. Interestingly, Baldwin notes,

> The offer of all kinds of adornment meant that prospective queens revealed by the choice they made whether they had good judgment and artistic sense, or whether they were interested only in enriching themselves.[59]

Her decision to take Hegai's advice proved a wise one.

Some women are unwilling to heed advice. Proverbs 12:15 states " . . . a wise man (or woman) listens to advice." Proverbs 19:20 instructs us to "Listen to advice and accept instruction, and in the end you will be wise." Esther even when elevated to the position of queen never got to the point of not needing advice from anyone. She was a humble woman who gained success through listening to wise advice. (See Chapter Three: Ruth)

A woman faced with a dilemma

> Mordecai told him everything that had happened to him, including the exact amount of money Haman promised to pay into the royal treasury for the destruction of the Jews. He also gave him a copy of the text of the edict for their annihilation, which had been published in Susa, to show to Esther and explain it to her, and he told him to urge her to go into the king's presence to beg for mercy and plead with him for her people. (Est. 4: 7-8)

All was going well for Esther. She lived a comfortable life where all her needs were met and she had little to worry about. However, life does not always run smoothly and soon Esther came face to face with a huge storm. Haman, one of the king's highest nobles, set in motion a plan to exterminate the Jews in the city of Susa. Mordecai, in much distress, reported to his cousin's attendant what was happening. Now Esther was in a difficult position. What should she do? She could continue to live a life of ease in the palace and not trouble herself with the problems of the people outside the gates. Nevertheless, she knew what she had to do, and emulated what other great saints had done before.

> By faith Moses, when he was grown up, refused to be called the son of Pharaoh's daughter, choosing rather to be mistreated with the people of God than to enjoy the fleeting pleasures of sin. He considered the reproach of Christ greater wealth than the treasures of Egypt, for he was looking to the reward. (Heb. 11:24-26)

Courageous

" . . . I will go to the king, even though it is against the law. And if I perish, I perish." (Est. 4:16)

Esther's faith in God is not unlike that of Shadrach, Meshach, and Abednego in the story of Daniel.

> If we are thrown into the blazing furnace, the God we serve is able to save us from it, and he will rescue us from your hand, O king. But even if he does not, we want you to know, O king, that we will not serve your gods or worship the image of gold you have set up. (Dan. 3:17-18)

It might have been easier for these three servants of God to give into the pressure of following the crowd and for the sake of personal safety to give in to worshipping the image of the king, but they refused. They chose instead to be faithful to God. Equally, Esther might have opted for an easier solution. Instead, Esther risked her life in order to speak up for her people at the right time. As a result, she saved the lives of the many Jews living in Persia. The easy route is not always the best route.

Esther was not naive but knew the possible outcome of her actions.

> All the king's officials and the people of the royal provinces know that for any man or woman who approaches the king in the inner court without being summoned the king has but one law: that he be put to death. The only exception to this is for the king to extend the gold sceptre to him and spare his life. But thirty days have passed since I was called to go to the king. (Est. 4:11)

Esther let it be known that she was aware that her action in approaching the king would go against the law of the land and she was unsure of her position with the king as he had shown little interest in her in recent times. There was real danger involved. Esther made the choice to risk her life to save others. *"Esther was willing to step into the unknown and risk her life. She would do her part, not knowing how the king would respond."*[60] Sometimes we have to do what is right despite the risks and the fear we may entertain and leave the consequences to God. Women of God we need to stand up and do what is right. There is a time to act—a time to stand up and be counted. Take courage! *"All that is necessary for evil to succeed is that good men do nothing."* (Attributed to Edmund Burke–a noted political thinker)

A woman of prayer

> Go, gather together all the Jews who are in Susa, and fast for me. Do not eat or drink for three days, night or day. I and my maids will fast as you do. (Est. 4:16)

Esther knew that she could not stand idly by and allow her people to perish. However, she knew also that before she could do anything, she needed the help and support of others. She knew the need to pray and the need to have God's mind on the matter. She needed God on her side if she was to win the favour of the king. She knew this was not a job for her alone. In a time of difficulty, Esther needed the mutual support of a caring, believing community. She did not try to go it alone but called on Mordecai and all the Jews to support her in prayer. She also involved her maids in this activity of prayer. This may suggest that she had already taught her maids about the God whom she served. Together in humble dependence on God, the situation would be resolved.

A woman of action

"In the third day Esther put on her royal robes and stood in the inner court of the palace, in front of the king's hall." (Est. 5:1)

Esther did not fall apart in the face of bad news but took action. She refused to allow the fear of a terrible situation to paralyse her. Psalm 112:7 states that a righteous man "will have no fear of bad news; his heart is steadfast, trusting in the LORD." Our fears subside in the knowledge that God is trustworthy. We all want to make a difference and the story of Esther shows us that we can. Esther acted with confidence, knowing that God was with her. When it is within our reach to save or help others, we must make every effort to do so.

A woman of wisdom

'If it pleases the king,' replied Esther, 'let the king, together with Haman, come today to a banquet I have prepared for him.' (Est. 5:4)

Esther thought carefully before she acted. She did not rush, but thought the matter through, making a wise plan of action. She knew the danger of approaching the king without an invitation, so she urged Mordecai to gather the Jews to fast, while she and her maids also set their minds to the task of fasting. She then dressed beautifully and stood in a conspicuous place where the king would notice her. He extended an invitation to her, and she then set her plan in motion. Esther invited the king and Haman (the enemy of the Jews) to a banquet. Her invitation was accepted, and they both came, but again Esther was prepared to wait a little longer and invited them to a second banquet the following day. It is then that she felt the time was right for her revelation. There is a time and place for everything, and we need to think carefully about the right time to reveal things. Patience to wait on the right timing is important when revealing matters of sensitivity (See Chapter Four: Abigail).

Concerned about other's welfare

Then Queen Esther answered, 'If I have found favour with you, O king, and if it pleases your majesty, grant me my life–this is my petition. And

> spare my people–this is my request. For I and my
> people have been sold for destruction and slaughter
> and annihilation . . . ' (Est. 7:3-4)

Esther's position of power did not overshadow her concern for others. Many who get to the top of their career or those who are elevated to high positions feather their own nests. They feel they have made it and are concerned only to better themselves. Esther used her position selflessly. Some might see such a position as an opportunity to be served, but Esther chose to use her position to serve others. Esther, when informed of the plight of her fellow Jews, did not close her eyes to their distress.

Many who find themselves in positions of power become immune or hard-hearted to the plight of others, but Esther preserved her compassion and concern for her fellow man. Many in this world look out for themselves. Selfish interests often take pride of place. "For everyone looks out for his own interests, not those of Jesus Christ." (Phil. 2:21) Esther knew that it was "better to be lowly in spirit and among the oppressed than to share the plunder of the proud." (Prov. 16:19) She identified with her people and their concerns became her concerns. At the right time, Queen Esther revealed those concerns to the king.

In the right place at the right time

"And who knows but that you have come to royal position for such a time as this." (Est. 4:14)

God had a plan to save his people from the wicked plot of the racist Haman and for that plan to be successful, he had a person in the right place at the right time. In the midst of racial hatred, God needed someone to thwart the destruction planned for God's chosen people. Esther was that person, as Mordecai suggested.

You may not understand why you are where you are, but God may be placing you there for an opportune time. Your present position of authority could enable you to act to save others' lives in a time of distress. Esther's strategic position of influence was put to good use for the benefit of others. At times, her life as one among many wives of the king may have appeared meaningless, but Esther was ready and available to God at the right time. She may have waited daily for the king's summons. However, on a deeper level than this, she was ready also for the summons of the King of kings. It is not clear how she filled her time. She may have wondered why God had allowed her to spend her days in apparent uselessness. Her life as one of many of the king's wives may not have been ideal, but Esther dealt graciously with a situation not of her choosing and was where God wanted her to be.

Prepared to be different

In Esther's day, women remained quiet and served at home. Women were not encouraged to play an active role in political matters. Generally, the same is true in Africa, though in recent times we have had some notable women involved in the political arena. Esther broke through the cultural norm and stepped beyond her culturally expected role to become a useful instrument in God's hand. We need to be available for God to use us to do what others might be afraid to do!

Rewarded for her courage and faithfulness

> On that day King Ahasuerus gave to Queen Esther the house of Haman, the enemy of the Jews. And Mordecai came before the king, for Esther had told what he was to her. And the king took off his signet ring, which he had taken from Haman, and gave it to Mordecai. And Esther set Mordecai over the house of Haman. (Est. 8:1-2 ESV)

On the day that Haman died for his wicked attempt to exterminate the Jews, the king rewarded Esther for her faithfulness and courage. Esther had sought the welfare of others and had reaped a reward.

Successful in averting the problems of her people

Having exposed the treachery of the wicked Haman, Esther was now given the opportunity to turn things around. The king gave her authority to write a new decree and to seal it with his ring of authority. This she did, giving the Jews the right to defend themselves against their enemies. As a result, "The Jews had light and gladness and joy and honour." (Est. 8:16) Through Esther and Mordecai, God had wiped away their tears. When the time came, the Jews took the necessary action to defend themselves, and refused to enrich themselves in the process. This action was very different to what the wicked Haman had planned. He had hoped not only to exterminate the Jews but also to enrich himself and the royal treasury in the process.

Esther showed that one with God was a majority. At times, we may be asked to act alone with courage and strength of character. May God give us such courage when asked to do so!

What lessons can we learn about God?

God is:

In control

"The LORD has established his throne in heaven, and his kingdom rules over all." (Ps. 103:19) Interestingly, God's name is not mentioned in the Book of Esther, but God's providential hand is clearly seen behind the scenes of Esther's life. Esther is specially positioned by God to be used to rescue God's people. The king's sleepless night; the reading of the chronicles; the failure to honour Mordecai earlier, the appearance of Haman in the court: God arranged all these things for the benefit of God's people. (Rom. 8:28) God causes people to rise and to fall from positions of responsibility. Esther was in the right place at the right time to be God's instrument of blessing to her people.

Able to overrule man's evil plans

> He who is pregnant with evil and conceives trouble
> gives birth to disillusionment. He who digs a hole
> and scoops it out falls into the pit he has made. (Ps.
> 7:14-15)

Because of God, Haman's plot to exterminate the Jews did not prosper. Haman's evil fell back on his own head. "Whoever digs a pit will fall into it, and a stone will come back on him who starts it rolling." (Prov. 26:27) God is able to turn around men's plans. By building a huge gallows, Haman determined to humiliate Mordecai. Instead, it was Haman who faced humiliation, for Haman had taken on a bigger opponent than he realised.

A deliverer

> The LORD is my rock, my fortress and my deliverer;
> my God is my rock, in whom I take refuge. He is my
> shield and the horn of my salvation, my stronghold.
> (Ps. 18:1-2)

God is able to deliver us from our enemies. We need have no fear of what men will do to us in the light of the powerful deliverances of God. God protects his people. Jews today still celebrate the feast of Purim, during which they recount the story of Esther. The feast is an annual reminder of God's great deliverance of his people.

Special Focus: Christ in the Story of Esther

Throughout the Old Testament lies the thread of the promise of Messiah. Esther's own life is intricately bound together with the threatened Jewish people. The threat against the Jews orchestrated by Haman was a threat against the promise of God concerning Messiah. If Haman had succeeded, then God would not have proved faithful to the promise of a Redeemer. Esther prevented such a calamity from happening. Thanks to Esther, God's plan and purpose were not thwarted. Jesus the Redeemer has come to save humanity from sin.

Even as Haman died on the very gallows he had erected for Mordecai, similarly the very cross on which he tried to destroy Jesus defeated Satan.

Since the children have flesh and blood, he too shared in their humanity so that by his death he might destroy him who holds the power of death–that is, the devil–and free those who all their lives were held in slavery by their fear of death. (Heb. 2:14-15)

Esther acted as a mediator between her people and the king. Jesus is our High priest who acts as our advocate and mediator between God and us. "For there is one God and one mediator between God and men, the man Christ Jesus . . ." (1 Tim. 2:5)

> You have come to God, the judge of all men, to the spirits of righteous men made perfect, to Jesus the mediator of a new covenant, to the sprinkled blood that speaks a better word than the blood of Abel. (Heb. 12:23-24)

For Further Discussion

1. Talk about times when you have sensed God's guiding hand behind the scenes in your life.

2. How do you think you might have responded if you had been in Esther's situation?

3. In light of the second decree, which gave the Jews the right to defend themselves, discuss the difference between self-defence and taking vengeance?

Chapter Seven
Anna - A Woman Who Met her Saviour.

(Ref. Luke 2: 36-38)

Name

Anna means 'Grace,'[61] just like the Old Testament name 'Hannah.'

Profile

- A prophetess.

- Daughter of Phanuel, of the tribe of Asher.

- A very old woman.

- Became a widow after seven years of marriage.

- No mention of any children.

Background

According to Jewish law, the male child was to be

circumcised on the eighth day. In accordance with this law, Mary and Joseph brought the baby Jesus to the temple. It was here that Anna met with Jesus, the 'Promised Messiah.'

What lessons can we learn from Anna's Life?

Anna was:

A prophetess

"There was also a prophetess, Anna, the daughter of Phanuel, of the tribe of Asher." (Luke 2:36)

Anna is introduced to us as a prophetess, that is, a spokesperson for God. She was someone who stood in the counsel of God and passed on his message to others. She was a true prophetess, appointed and sent by God with the truth and not a self-appointed prophetess, who spoke from her own imaginings. (See Chapter Two: Deborah)

Anna was a useful instrument in God's hand. As she witnessed the presentation of the baby Jesus at the Temple, she added her own prophetic voice to Simeon's, acknowledging that Jesus was indeed the promised Messiah, the hope of Israel. Simeon, a righteous and devout man had recognised this blessed baby and had declared wondrous things concerning him, much to the parents' surprise. However, God had more surprises in store for them as Simeon's testimony was strengthened further by the voice of Anna, God's prophetess.

It is as if Anna is the second witness confirming the truth about Jesus' identity, for based on two or three witnesses, truths are established. (see also Deut. 17:6; Matt. 18:16; 2 Cor. 13:1 and 1 Tim. 5:19)[62] Anna gave witness to the 'faithful and true witness.' (Rev. 3:14) "The testimony of these witnesses adds to the collage of heavenly and earthly voices that have spoken up for Jesus."[63] In this world, plenty of voices speak out against Christ and Christianity, but Anna is faithful in testifying to who Jesus is.

A very old woman

"She was very old" or "She was advanced in years." (Luke 2:36 ESV)

Anna was past her prime and perhaps past what most people would consider her best years of usefulness. Nevertheless, Anna did not let her old age stand in the way of service for God. There is no doubt that as she aged, Anna knew her limits. She could not physically do all that she did when she was younger. However, Anna was still energetic and passionate for God. She had not allowed the years to dampen her spirit. She was on fire for God.

Anna was like the picture painted of the righteous person in the Psalms.

> The righteous will flourish like a palm tree, they will grow like a cedar of Lebanon; planted in the house of the LORD, they will flourish in the courts of our God. They will still bear fruit in old age, they will stay fresh and green, proclaiming, 'The LORD is upright; he is my Rock, and there is no wickedness in him.' (Ps. 92:14)

Many people facing old age begin to think that they are past their age of usefulness. They do not have the strength they once had. However, none of this seemed to bother Anna. She continued to bear fruit in her old age and to trust in God for daily strength.

In this scene at the Temple, the elderly Simeon and Anna play a significant and complementary role. They, along with others present, are given the honour of sharing in the joy of Messiah's arrival. They are not pushed into the background for Jesus has come for all mankind, for male and female, for young and old, for all who would call on his name.[64] As Bentley states, Anna because of her gender and status in society *"was not a very likely candidate to have the honour of meeting the King of kings."*[65]

Anna refused to give up living while she was still alive. She continued to be a living, vibrant messenger of God and as a result, Anna lived a fulfilling, rewarding life. She chose to live out her days in service to God. She lived a purpose-filled old age, not just sitting in her house awaiting death, as some do.

Our old age could be used more judiciously. Anna used her old age to continue to proclaim God's wonders and praise. Whereas for Simeon seeing the Christ child provided closure to his earthly life, for Anna the same event triggered a new beginning, as she boldly proclaimed the Messiah's arrival to all who would listen.[66]

Proverbs 16:29 declares "Grey hair is a crown of splendour; it is attained by a righteous life." The people of Israel believed that a long life was a sign of God's blessing. Old people can rejoice in their years of experience and practical wisdom. Grey hair is not a disgrace, and the older members of our communities deserve to be treated with respect. Young people need to remember *"an old banana leaf was once young and green."* (Nigerian Proverb)

In Africa, generally old age is applauded. A long life is celebrated. The elderly are respected, honoured, and taken care of. They are the people of wisdom and experience in the community. It is good when old people contribute these gifts of old age back into society.

However, things are changing for old people in Africa and measures need to be put in place to protect these vulnerable members of our society. Traditionally the extended family took responsibility for those who were no longer able to engage in economic activity due to old age. Factors such as globalisation, urbanisation and the HIV/AIDS crisis are having a huge negative impact on African society. In fact, it is often the case that an increasing burden of care for younger members of the family is now being placed on the elderly. *The notion that 'we take care of our elders' is still often heard but is increasingly not reflected in reality.*[67]

God's word instructs us to respect and take care of the elderly. "Rise in the presence of the aged, show respect for the elderly and revere your God. I am the LORD." (Lev. 19:32) How we treat others shows what we really think of God. If we respect and take care of the elderly, we show reverence to God. Both go hand in hand.

> Don't be harsh or impatient with an older man. Talk
> to him as you would your own father . . . Reverently
> honour an older woman as you would your mother
> . . . (1 Tim. 5:1-2 MSG)

A widow

> . . . she had lived with her husband seven years
> after her marriage, and then was a widow until she
> was eighty-four. (Luke 2:36-37)

Unfortunately, life had dealt a big blow to Anna early on in her married life. She had enjoyed a partner for only seven years before he was taken away. It would appear that her husband had died too soon, before his time. However, Anna did not blame God and turn away from him. Her whole-hearted devotion to God left no room for bitterness to take root. *"Someone has said that trouble can make a person bitter or better. It's clear that loss and sorrow and deprivation made Anna better."*[68] She believed like Job that the Lord had the right to give and the right to take away at his own time and for his own purpose. (Job 1:21) Anna had suffered a devastating loss but remained strong in faith. She forgot her troubles and kept her eyes fixed on God. She responded to calamity by placing her future in God's hands. She was a widow for over sixty years yet remained steadfast in devotion to God.

Anna handled her sorrow well and kept her focus on the immoveable, unchangeable God. Her life had changed dramatically with the death of her husband, but Anna had survived intact, having kept her faith in God. She overcame the reproach of widowhood and God had become her husband. "For your Maker is your husband—the LORD Almighty is his name . . ." (Isa. 54:5)

Anna trusted God and cast her burdens on to God. She had someone to turn to when her earthly partner had left this physical world. There is no doubt that she mourned his passing, but Anna did not fall to pieces or become addicted to too much wine, nor did she jump from one man's bed to another in search of companionship.

The plight of widows is a real one in Africa where many are faced with the prospect of having to marry a brother of the deceased or are faced with being thrown out of the husband's home. Often a widow is accused of her husband's death. To add to her grief, children are sometimes taken away. (See Chapter Three: Ruth) We do not know what Anna faced, but it appears that her earthly troubles drew her nearer to God and not further away.

Anna invested her time wisely. She does not appear to have been a busybody or gossip. Speaking of younger widows Paul warns Timothy that they can tend to

> . . . get into the habit of being idle and going about from house to house. And not only do they become idlers, but also gossips and busybodies, saying things they ought not to. (1 Tim. 5:13)

To her credit, Anna had refused to become such a person though widowed at a young age.

The church needs to respond to the needs of widows. (1 Tim. 5:3-5) Anna and others like her ought to be respected and honoured in our communities. Widows themselves should seek to be in fellowship with other believers, for God sets the lonely in families. (Ps. 68:5-6) Isolation is not a good thing. Like embers in a fire, when taken out of the fire, the flame soon quenches, so we need to be joined together with other believers so that we will continue to thrive. Fellowship with God and fellowship with other believers is vital.

Content

Anna like the apostle Paul learned the secret of contentment.

> I have learned the secret of being content in any and every situation, whether well fed or hungry, whether living in plenty or in want. I can do everything through him who gives me strength. (Phil. 4:12-13)

When life's trials threaten to pull the mat from under our feet, how do we find our balance again? Anna found hers in the Lord, her solid rock, her hiding place. Like the psalmist, Anna found shelter and rest in the "shadow of the Almighty." (Ps. 91:1)

A worshipper

"She never left the temple but worshipped night and day, fasting and praying." (Luke 2:37)

Anna spent her life worshipping, praying and fasting, day in and day out in the Temple. This was where Anna had made her home, that is, in the presence of God. She devoted her entire existence to God and to his service. She would rather be in the presence of the Lord than anywhere else.

Worship certainly was not a Sunday affair for Anna. She was concerned to be in the presence of God, twenty-four hours a day and seven days a week. Many think worship is for Sundays only. However, God wants a living vibrant relationship with his people, one that carries on throughout the working week. God wants to be involved in our lives on a continual basis. God's word instructs us to pray continually. (1 Thess. 5:17) As Paul wrote to Timothy, he spoke of a widow like Anna.

> The widow who is really in need and left all alone
> puts her hope in God and continues night and day
> to pray and to ask God for help. (1 Tim. 5:5)

Anna had no one else to depend on, but who better to depend on than the God "who owns the cattle on a thousand hills?" (Ps. 50:10)

Anna did not see her widowhood as an impediment but used the extra time on her hands to serve God unhindered. Her declaration was like that of Asaph in Psalm 73:25 "Whom have I in heaven, but you?" Anna was a faithful disciplined woman given to daily and consistent worship of God.

In tune with God

> Coming up to them at that very moment, she gave thanks to God and spoke about the child to all who were looking forward to the redemption of Jerusalem. (Luke 2: 38)

When Anna saw the infant Jesus, God's Spirit in her opened her eyes to recognise the long-expected Messiah. She had waited a long time for this moment. She had no idea how it would happen, but this was it: God's plan of salvation unfolding itself before her very eyes. She may have wondered many times what this Christ of God might look like and here he was for all to see. She had waited long, not giving up and finally her perseverance had paid off. She had prayed for this long-expected day.

Anna knew how to wait; and that's why as a woman whose credentials might seem to fit on a pinhead, she has found an esteemed place in the sacred story. She wrote no books, performed no concerts, was elected to no office, but the Church knows her as a saint.[69]

Anna, like Simeon, had longed to see the Messiah, had longed for Israel's redemption. "Without notice or invitation cards, Simeon and Anna meet at the right moments by the intuition of the Holy Spirit."[70]

Anna was the first woman to publicly recognise and acknowledge Jesus Christ as the Messiah, the Anointed One of God. Truly all things had worked together for good. God had preserved her for this very day. She saw the positives of her situation and not the negatives. Her faithfulness and devotion had brought its reward. She was privileged to be present to witness the presentation of Jesus at the Temple. Anna from the family of Phanuel (Peniel, meaning the face of God) had literally seen the face of God in this baby. In the ordinary habits of her life, one ordinary day became extraordinary as she recognised the Saviour.

No doubt having lost her precious partner, she had known times of great sadness, but God had restored her joy and, on this day, her joy was made full, for she had witnessed the Saviour of the world. Her hope had not been in vain. This was a wonderful day, as God fulfilled his long-awaited promise.

Thankful

" . . . she began to give thanks to God . . ." (Luke 2:38 ESV)

Anna gave thanks. The One in whom she had put her trust had not disappointed her. He had heard her prayers and had answered her petitions. She acknowledged God's answer to her prayers and gave him the thanks due to his name.

Anna's thankfulness no doubt stemmed from a life of thankfulness. Such thankfulness ought to be the mark of the Christian life. Ephesians 5:4 exhorts us "Let there be no filthiness nor foolish talk nor crude joking, which are out of place, but instead let there be thanksgiving." Equally Ephesians 5:20 states " . . . giving thanks always for everything to God the Father in the name of our Lord Jesus Christ." Anna's words of thankfulness reflected a thankful heart.

An evangelist

" . . . and spoke about the child to all who were looking forward to the redemption of Jerusalem." (Luke 2:38)

Having recognised Jesus, she immediately began to introduce him to those who were longing for the redemption of Jerusalem. She was the first woman to proclaim the truth about Christ to the people around her. She did not allow her gender to hold her back and she did not hold her tongue, believing that the work of evangelism was for men alone. She did not make excuses because of her old age or lack of rabbinic training. She was thrilled to introduce Christ to others and to proclaim the Good News of God's salvation to the people.

What lessons can we learn about God?

God is:

A protector of widows

"A father to the fatherless, a defender of widows is God in his holy dwelling." (Ps. 68:5) God is especially concerned for the weak and vulnerable. "He defends the cause of the fatherless and the widow . . ." (Deut. 10:18)

Faithful

> Know therefore that the LORD your God is God; he is the faithful God, keeping his covenant of love to a thousand generations of those who love him and keep his commands. (Deut. 7:9)

God had lovingly sustained Anna through many years of life as a widow and he can do the same for us in times of need for he is dependable and trustworthy. He does not disappoint.

Worthy of our devotion

"For great is the LORD and most worthy of praise; he is to be feared above all gods." (1 Chron. 16:25) Anna lived a life of devotion to God. She is an example for us to follow. She delighted in her God and he delighted in her. In the absence of a husband, God became her husband, her soul mate, and her closest companion.

A communicator and revealer of mysteries

> Daniel replied, 'No wise man, enchanter, magician or diviner can explain to the king the mystery he has asked about, but there is a God in heaven who reveals mysteries.' (Dan. 2:2-28)

Just as God, years before, revealed things to Daniel, God also revealed to Anna that the baby in the Temple was the Messiah for whom she had been waiting. God reveals his secrets to his servants. Let us be ever ready to hear his voice. "O my people, hear my teaching; listen to the words of my mouth." (Ps. 78:1)

A rewarder of faithfulness

> And without faith it is impossible to please God, because anyone who comes to him must believe that

he exists and that he rewards those who earnestly seek him. (Heb. 11:6)

God rewarded this devoted servant with the ultimate prize, the opportunity to witness the Messiah in the flesh. God's word encourages us not to give up. Anna did not grow weary or lose heart and her reward was great.

Therefore, since we are surrounded by such a great cloud of witnesses, let us throw off everything that hinders and the sin that so easily entangles, and let us run with perseverance the race marked out for us. Let us fix our eyes on Jesus, the author and perfecter of our faith, who for the joy set before him endured the cross, scorning its shame, and sat down at the right hand of the throne of God. (Heb. 12:1-2) Keep on keeping on!

A promise keeper

. . . You know with all your heart and soul that not one of all the good promises the LORD your God gave you has failed. Every promise has been fulfilled; not one has failed. (Josh. 23:14)

God had promised to send the Messiah. Anna had prayed and longed for his coming and now she had witnessed the fulfilment of God's promise. Anna, just like Joshua, knew that her God had faithfully kept his promises.

Special Focus: Christ in the Story of Anna

Christ became one of us so that he could identify with mankind and act as our substitute, taking our sins upon himself. He came as a vulnerable baby subject to the limitations of the human frame and subject to the requirements of the Jewish law. Jesus was born in a humble stable to a poor family and was presented in the Temple along with the offering of "a pair of doves or two young pigeons." (Luke 2:24)

> For you know the grace of our Lord Jesus Christ, that though he was rich, yet for your sakes he became poor, so that you through his poverty might become rich. (2 Cor. 8:9)

Apart from Simeon and Anna many did not recognise who Jesus was. As Anna proclaimed him as the Redeemer, many may have thought that she had lost her mind, but the opposite was true for she saw correctly that Jesus was indeed the Saviour of the world. "And we have seen and testify that the Father has sent his Son to be the Saviour of the world." (I John 4:14)

For Further Discussion

1. "Devote yourselves to prayer being watchful and thankful." (Col. 4:2) To what extent has this become a reality in your life? Why is prayer so important?

2. What have you learned from Anna's life that might help in times of separation from or loss of a loved one?

3. Think about practical ways to encourage older people so that they can make a positive contribution in their communities.

Chapter Eight
Mary Magdalene - A Woman Who Was Thankful

(Ref: Matt. 27: 55-56, 61; 28:1; Mark 15:40-41, 47, 16:1-11;

Luke 8: 1-3; 23:49; 23:55-24:11; John 19:25; 20:1-18)

Name

The name 'Mary' comes from the name of the herb 'myrrh,' which is a bitter healing herb, used in medicines and perfume.[71] It was a common name at the time.[72]

Profile

- A woman from whom seven spirits were cast out.

- Appears to have been a wealthy woman.

- Came from a place called Magdala, by the Sea of Galilee.

Background

Magdala was not far from Nazareth, Jesus' home place and Jesus may have gone there several times. It was a thriving fishing village. On one of these occasions, it is supposed that he met Mary and healed her of her condition of demon possession. The events of the cross, resurrection and ascension took place about A.D. 30. [73]

What lessons can we learn from Mary's life?

Mary was:

A disciple

> After this, Jesus travelled about from one town and village to another, proclaiming the good news of the kingdom of God. The Twelve were with him, and also some women who had been cured of evil spirits and diseases: Mary (called Magdalene) from whom seven demons had come out; Joanna the wife of Cuza, the manager of Herod's household; Susanna; and many others. These women were helping to support them out of their own means. (Luke 8:1-3)

Mary was amongst many women who followed Jesus. She travelled in the company of Jesus and his disciples. This was the greatest example of discipleship—leaving all to follow Christ. Mary Magdalene and these other women chose to leave behind the comfort of home to suffer along with Christ as he moved about proclaiming the gospel. These women had witnessed the power and love of God in their own lives. They had believed his message and now their lives were dedicated to following Christ. They were not ashamed of the gospel, and neither were they afraid to be associated with Jesus. Women in Jesus' day played a vital role in his ministry, and they still play a vital role today in Jesus' ministry through the church.

A loving and caring woman

"These women were helping to support them out of their own means." (Luke 8:3) "Many women were there, watching from a distance. They had followed Jesus from Galilee to care for his needs!" (Matt. 27:55)

Not just during his times of active service, but in his last hours these ladies were there. Mary is mentioned amongst a group of women who were dedicated to serving their Master and supplying his needs along with those of his disciples. For Mary, this was a loving act for a Master who had done the impossible for her. Before she met the Lord, she had lived a dreadful life subject to the torment of seven demons. People subject to demons were not only victims of the demons who possessed them, but also outcasts of the community in which they lived. Many would have looked at Mary as a crazy woman, a woman to avoid, yet the Master had shown compassion on her, had completely healed her and she was grateful. Her service was the least she could give to show her appreciation to her Lord. She had found love and understanding, and she was not going to give that up easily. She was like the merchant who found a pearl of great value "he went away and sold everything he had and bought it." (Matt. 13:46) Mary had traded in her old life for a new life of dedication to the One who truly loved her.

A former demoniac

> . . . and also some women who had been cured of
> evil spirits and diseases: Mary (called Magdalene)
> from whom seven demons had come out (Luke 8:2).

The character of Mary Magdalene is often associated with that of the sinful woman, a lady with a history of sexual sin, but in fact this cannot be proven.[74] Mary indeed had a history, but it appears to have involved demons and not necessarily sexual sin. The truth declared clearly in the Scriptures is that Jesus set Mary free from demon possession. The mention of 'seven' demons seems to suggest that her condition had been a very serious one. She had lived a life of intolerable affliction, but God had set her free. She had lived a life filled with torment, now her life was filled with peace and wellbeing.

Some people are afflicted with mental illness, which can stem from a variety of causes. In African societies, some people believe that evil spirits or curses inflict mental illness. Whatever the cause, there is a stigma that surrounds mental illness. Those with mental illness often face a negative attitude, rather than a sympathetic one. Many fear mental illness and victims are often chained (to keep them from harming themselves or others), beaten and abused. People with mental problems, or who are subject to demon possession, are avoided and treated as social outcasts. Much of this negative treatment arises from a lack of knowledge and a general attitude of fear towards those who do not appear to be behaving normally. Furthermore, there is often a lack of access to medical treatment, which does not help the situation.

Mary's case shows us that those who suffer from mental disturbance can find healing. While Mary's mental problems were caused by demons, it is important to note that demons are not the sole cause of all mental illness. There may be physical causes, chemical imbalances in the system or other spiritual conditions that stimulate mental problems. The cause of mental instability will affect the type of treatment administered.

Jesus did not fear Mary or her condition but drew near and brought soundness of mind to her, by expelling the demons that had inhabited her life. Mental illness, whatever its cause, can be treated and the person can live a productive life. The Christian community needs to learn more about mental illness and needs to approach those afflicted, with sympathy, rather than condemnation. Jesus took time to treat Mary and as a result, Mary became a dedicated follower of Jesus and a productive member of her community.

Prayer is a key element in the healing of those afflicted with demons.

> After Jesus had gone indoors, his disciples asked him privately, 'Why couldn't we drive it out?' He replied, 'This kind can come out only by prayer (and fasting).' (Mark 9:28-29)

In other words, this case of demon possession needed dedication and effort in prayer. We are not told how Mary was healed but no doubt, prayer was a key element.

A thankful woman with a servant heart

Mary Magdalene is often placed first in a list of women who cared for Jesus and his disciples' needs. It would appear that she played a leading role in serving them. She was a hard-working lady, committed to playing her part in her Saviour's ministry.

Mary had witnessed the power and love of God in action. Therefore, it appears that in grateful response, Mary now used every opportunity to demonstrate her thankfulness in practical ways. She was grateful and sought ways to give something back to Jesus. Mary did not need to be taught to serve, but service flowed from a heart of thankfulness.

> Each one should use whatever gift he has received to serve others, faithfully administering God's grace in its various forms. If anyone speaks, he should do it as one speaking the very words of God. If anyone serves, he should do it with the strength God provides, so that in all things God may be praised through Jesus Christ. (1 Pet. 4:10-11)

A wealthy woman

"These women were helping to support them out of their own means." (Luke 8:3)

Mary used her wealth for the relief of others' needs. Mary had lived as a demoniac, but she was now clothed and in her right mind. Before this time, demons had controlled her, now she submitted willingly to Christ's loving authority. She lived for him. She devoted her heart, her life, her time and her wealth to the Lord. She held nothing back and was willing to share all she had with others. God gives us the ability to gain wealth and he expects us to use that wealth wisely and generously. (1 Tim. 6:17-19) (See Chapter Four: Abigail)

Loyal to the end

"Mary Magdalene and Mary, the mother of Joses saw where he was laid." (Mark 15:47)

Mary was not only a follower of Jesus but was wholeheartedly devoted to him. Mary was not stingy in her devotion but withheld nothing from God. She loved him truly with all her soul, all her mind, and all her strength. Mary was not worried about associating herself with Christ, for he was the one she loved and adored. He supported her and was not ashamed to be associated with her. In turn, she remained firm, and though it was difficult to watch her Master die, she resolved to follow him to the end. As Kalas notes *"Great souls prove their greatness in the darkest of times."*[75]

During the days of busy ministry life, Mary was there. When Jesus was questioned and tried by the authorities, Mary was there. When Jesus was crucified, Mary was there. Mary stood at the cross when many fled in fear of their lives. She was not afraid to be near Christ. She did not abandon him, as he died the death of a condemned criminal. Mary remained close to her Master. When Jesus was buried, Mary was there. Mary was there, loyal to her Master until she was sure there was nothing more she could do for him. This dogged loyalty was met with reward as Mary became the first witness to see the risen Lord.

A witness of the resurrection

"When Jesus rose early on the first day of ther week, he appeared first to Mary Magdalene . . ." (Mark 16:9)

Early in the morning while it was still dark Mary

went to the tomb. Whereas the disciples came and went, Mary stayed weeping. Mary could not leave until she found answers. As far as she was concerned, she had lost her most treasured possession. She wanted to care for Jesus unto the end but because the body was missing, she had been denied the opportunity of this last service to her Lord and Master. Her distress came from the fact that she did not know where Jesus' body was. However, her sadness soon turned to joy.

> They came to the tomb expecting to find the death of their hopes, but now everything is turned upside down, and even their wildest dreams pale beside the astonishing message that Jesus has been raised.[76]

Therefore, when Jesus appeared it was like a personal reunion with Mary. She saw a man standing there and

> Thinking he was the gardener, she said, 'Sir, if you have carried him away, tell me where you have put him, and I will get him.' Jesus said to her, 'Mary.' (John. 20:15)

Mary would treasure these moments of intimacy with her Master for years to come. She was honoured to be the first person to see the risen Lord. Mary may have suffered from low self-esteem having spent many years as an outcast of her society. Not now, for Jesus had entrusted her with the most important message of all time.

Since the women are present for Jesus' death on the cross and his burial by Joseph of Arimathea (see also 27:55-56, 61), they can verify that Jesus is truly dead, not just unconscious. God is bestowing a special honour on them. They are exemplary of true discipleship to Jesus, and because of their faithfulness and courage, they are given the special honour of being witnesses to these profound events.[77]

A woman faced with change

"Jesus said, 'Do not hold on to me, for I have not yet returned to the Father.'" (John 20:17)

Mary did not want her relationship with Jesus to change. She had followed him faithfully. He had died and now miraculously he was standing before her alive. She wanted to hold on to things as they had been for so long. However, for her sake and for our sakes, things were about to change.

Jesus would return to the Father, but Mary desired to hold on to him, not to let him out of her sight.

Change is not always easy but is sometimes necessary for growth. Mary's loss of Christ's occasional earthly presence would be replaced by his constant spiritual presence. For the greater good, Mary had to let him go.

An apostle

> Mary Magdalene went to the disciples with the news: "I have seen the Lord!" And she told them that he had said these things to her. (John 20:18)

Though this title often applies, only to the twelve apostles I use the term in the sense of 'one who was a witness of Jesus' earthly ministry, death and resurrection and was sent by Jesus with the news of his resurrection.' Augustine wrote, *"The Holy Spirit made Magdalene the apostle of the apostles."*[78] The word 'apostle' can be interpreted as 'messenger, delegate or sent one.'[79] Jesus revealed himself first to Mary and appointed her to go and tell the others that he was alive. Jesus entrusted the central truth of the Christian faith to her, and she went willingly with this message.

> Jesus' intention in directing these women to call for his brothers to meet him in Galilee makes an important salvation-historical turning point. Since they are the first witnesses to the resurrection, this

> suggests that they should be regarded as equal in value to men and be restored as co-workers with men in the community of faith, a role they had been assigned from creation (Gen. 1:26-28).[80]

It seems that Jesus' choice of Mary as the messenger of the resurrection was intentional. He chose Mary for this special task. Ironically, the disciples were not impressed with what she said. They dismissed her message, believing it to be 'nonsense,' the mere ramblings of a mad person. "But they did not believe the women, because their words seemed to them like nonsense." (Luke 24:11) "When they heard that Jesus was alive and that she had seen him, they did not believe it." (Mark 16:11)

Maybe they thought Mary was still a little crazy. Maybe they thought there were still parts of her mind affected by her old life of demon possession. Of all people, the Lord would hardly choose a former mad woman to handle the greatest truth of all time, but he did. The past was the past, and this redeemed woman who was wholeheartedly devoted to her Lord, was the perfect messenger of the resurrection message. Jesus made no mistake.

Mary was not the foolish one here, but the disciples were. Mary no doubt was used to being misunderstood. This did not perturb her. She knew what she had witnessed and there was no doubt in her mind. She had seen Jesus with her own eyes and he had called her by name. 'Jesus was alive' whether the disciples chose to believe her words or not. She was only doing her job and passing on her Master's message. If the men refused to believe, they were the losers. In fact, because of their unbelief, they later faced the Master's rebuke,

> Later Jesus appeared to the Eleven as they were eating; he rebuked them for their lack of faith and their stubborn refusal to believe those who had seen him after he had risen. (Mark 16:14)

At a time when women's testimony held little weight in the culture of the day, Jesus sent this woman to testify of him to others. In doing so, Jesus elevated the status of women. God was saying that women could be trusted with important responsibilities. God used this woman to proclaim his truth and still uses women today in the proclamation of his message.

What lessons can we learn about God?

God is:

The great healer

> Praise the LORD, O my soul and forget not all his benefits—who forgives all your sins and heals all your diseases, who redeems your life from the pit and crowns you with love and compassion. (Ps. 103:2-4)

God is concerned about our well-being. He longs to make us whole and is concerned about those things that afflict us. Exodus 15:26 states, " . . . for I am the LORD, who heals you." God can and does heal, but sometimes God in his divine will does not always answer as we think he should. God's healing is for the praise of his glory.

Aware of our names

> But he who enters by the door is the shepherd of the sheep. To him the gatekeeper opens. The sheep hear his voice, and he calls his own sheep by name and leads them out. (John 10:2-3)

Jesus knew Mary inside out. He knew her heart and knew her by name. God knows us individually and by name. We may feel like a particularly small fish in a big pond, but nothing escapes God's notice. He is intimately acquainted with us.

> O LORD, you have searched me and you know me.
> You know when I sit and when I rise; You perceive
> my thoughts from afar. You discern my going out
> and my lying down; you are familiar with all my
> ways. Before a word is on my tongue you know it
> completely, O LORD. (Ps. 139:1-4)

One who rewards our devotion

"Come near to God and he will come near to you." (James 4:8) When we draw close to God, He draws close to us. We need to cling to our God even as Mary clung to Jesus. She was single-hearted in her devotion and God rewarded her with the responsibility of being the apostle of the resurrection message.

Special Focus: Christ in the Story of Mary Magdalene

Jesus is the Friend of the Despised.

When Mary was in her former state no one would have gone near, but Jesus did for he is the friend not only of the worst sinner but of the outcast; those who are rejected and despised by society. He is also the Great Healer.

> Jesus went through all the towns and villages,
> teaching in their synagogues, preaching the good

news of the kingdom and healing every disease and sickness. (Matt. 9:35)

Jesus is the Resurrection and the Life. (John 11:15)

Jesus' resurrection was testified to not only by Mary but by many witnesses. Because Jesus has risen, we will also rise. "But Christ has indeed been raised from the dead, the first fruits of those who have fallen asleep." (1 Cor. 15:20) Jesus' resurrection is at the core of the Christian message.

Jesus is the great Apostle.

Therefore, holy brothers, who share in the heavenly calling, fix your thoughts on Jesus, the apostle and high priest whom we confess. (Heb. 3:1)

God the Father sent Jesus Christ into this world. Jesus was the Message, the very Word of God the Father. (see also John 3:17, 34; 5:36-38; 6:29)

For Further Discussion

1. Because of what Jesus did for Mary, she responded in whole-hearted devotion and love to her Lord. How does such love challenge your own love for Jesus, considering what he has done for you?

2. Jesus spoke to Mary and gave her the important message of the resurrection to bring to her brothers. Does Jesus still speak through women today? Would you consider encouraging women who are gifted to use their gift in the church?

3. Why is the resurrection so important to the Christian faith? (Read 1 Cor. 15)

Chapter Nine
Sapphira–A Woman Who Lied to God

(Ref. Acts 5: 1-10)

Name

Sapphira means 'Beautiful.'[81]

Profile

- A believer in the early church at Jerusalem.

- Married to Ananias.

- No mention of children.

Background

The events of Ananias and Sapphira's lives take place at the early stages of the growth of the Christian church between A.D. 30 and A.D. 35.[82]

What lessons can we learn from Sapphira's life?

Sapphira was:

Deceitful

> Now a man named Ananias, together with his wife
> Sapphira, also sold a piece of property. With his
> wife's full knowledge, he kept back part of the
> money for himself, but brought the rest and put it at
> the apostles' feet. (Acts 5:1-2)

Not all wives know their husband's business. Many are, unfortunately, unaware of their husband's activities and many husbands are content to keep it that way. Often, there is little communication between husband and wife, despite the fact that God has designed them to be 'one.' Thus, when a business venture collapses, the woman is totally unprepared for the devastation that may follow. Perhaps a wise word from her at an earlier stage could have prevented the matter escalating to such a devastating point. "Plans fail for lack of counsel, but with many advisers they succeed." (Prov. 15:22)

However, Sapphira was in the unique position of not only knowing fully what her husband was doing but was directly involved in the selling of the piece of land. Sapphira could not stand back and say she did not know. She was fully aware. She could have advised her husband to do otherwise, but she does not seem to have objected to his underhand actions. Some women know quite well that their husbands are not doing what is right and fail to advise them, for many reasons.

Some fear their husbands' temper and choose the option to 'keep the peace' rather than provoke their husbands to anger. As women of God, we need to fear God more than man. "Fear of man will prove to be a snare, but whoever trusts in the LORD is kept safe." (Prov. 29:25) Some do not object to their husband's plans because they themselves do not regard sin as a serious matter. They see no harm in a little twisting of the truth. However, the seriousness of Sapphira's punishment alerts us to the fact that God does not take lying lightly. Some women suffer from low self-esteem. They do not value their own opinions, thinking they have little of significance to contribute. Women need to know that both men and women have been made in the image of God, so each person is of value and a woman's opinion is as valuable as anyone else's. Some women are victims of wrong beliefs. They may believe that submission to a husband means to submit in everything, whether good or bad. However, a wife has no obligation to obey her husband when it goes against the clearly revealed will of God. Sometimes women do not want to take responsibility for bad decisions and feel it is safer to make no decision at all. However, God gives women also the 'mind of Christ' and wisdom to make right choices.

As wives, we need to remember that we are our husband's helpmeet, that is, a suitable helper for him. One way we can help him is to assist him to become the man that God has called him to be. We can do this by supporting him in making wise and godly decisions. We may offer insight and solutions that our husbands have not thought of. Often women have insight that a man does not have. I remember when we were planning our wedding that one man gave my husband a word of advice. He said, *"Listen to your wife. There are things that she will know that you do not know. I don't know how she knows it, but trust me, she does."* Do not be afraid to advise your husbands. Your advice might even save them a lot of grief.

Concerned with outward appearances

> Joseph, a Levite from Cyprus, whom the apostles called Barnabas (which means Son of Encouragement), sold a field he owned and brought the money and put it at the apostles' feet. (Acts 4:36)

No one pressurised or even asked Ananias and Sapphira to sell their land and give the money to the church. It was not a requirement of membership of the new community of believers. However, others were doing it. It seems that Ananias and Sapphira succumbed to the pressure of looking good in others' eyes. They were more concerned with outward appearances than with purity of heart. Perhaps they thought people would be impressed if they sold land and seemingly gave all to the church. It would look like they were truly committed to both God and the church. They longed to hear the applause of men. People would look on admiringly and say, *"Well done!"* Perhaps they thought that this was a way of making their name great, or of moving to a place of prominence within the church. However, they should have learned from the lessons of Scripture that setting out to make one's name great usually ends in disaster. (see also Gen. 11:1-8)

It is very easy to fall into this trap especially during times of launching or public fund raising. Do we give with the right motive? If we are standing up to give so that people will admire us, then we are not giving in a right way. If we look for man's approval, then we have already received our reward. We ought not to expect any reward from God for our giving in that fashion.

> So when you give to the needy, do not announce it with trumpets, as the hypocrites do in the synagogues and on the streets, to be honoured by men. I tell you the truth, they have received their reward in full. (Matt. 6:2)

We are not to give, to make ourselves look good, but the kind of giving that God likes is cheerful giving, secret giving and giving without expecting anything in return.

Tempted by Satan

When the work of God is making progress, there is often a counterattack from Satan. As the fledgling church was making progress, 'an act of deceit' put a spanner in the works.[83] Ananias and Sapphira fell foul to Satan's schemes. When we come under God's rule, Satan is not happy. Even though Christ has already defeated him he will wage war against us. (1 Pet. 5:8-9) All Christians, especially those who are in the front line of Christian ministry, are open to attack. But God is our help and our strength and has given us his "sword of the Spirit, which is the word of God." (Eph. 6:17)

Sapphira was overcome by temptation and allowed

Satan the upper hand. Let us be wise and learn from her story. Sapphira knew about the sale of the land, and agreed to the plan to deceive the church leaders. She chose to participate in her husband's wrongdoing, rather than to do what was right. We need to be careful of the choices we make, for we will have no one to blame but ourselves.

Involved in misappropriation of funds

"With his wife's full knowledge, he kept back part of the money for himself." (Acts 5:2)

Ananias, in agreement with his wife, kept back some of the money for their own use. The words *'kept back'* are translated from the Greek *'nosphizo'* which means to misappropriate or embezzle.[84] (see also Titus 2:10) There would have been nothing wrong with keeping back some, as it was their money, but because they had lied and pretended that they were giving it all, it then became a case of misappropriation of funds. They brought only a part of the money and withheld some for themselves. Their greed got the better of them. I can just imagine the conversation between them.

Ananias: Sapphira, I have been thinking. I know we originally planned to give all this money to the church, but we actually got more than expected for the sale of the land. I was thinking that since we have some needs of our own and it is our money anyway, well maybe we should not give all. What do you think?

Sapphira: Well darling, the same thought was going through my mind. It seems too much just to hand over in one go. Anyway, how do we know if the others who sold land did not keep some for themselves? Even the leaders are new to this work, maybe it is not sensible to hand it all over. It seems wise to save some for ourselves for a rainy day.

Ananias: Yes, I think we will hold on to some for our own use. However, I think we should tell them that what we are giving is all of it. Well, it would look better that way. It would just look and sound better if we said we were sacrificially giving it all away. People would think more of us.

Sapphira: Yes, it might not sound the best if we were to say that we decided to hold on to some for ourselves. It certainly sounds better if it appears that we are giving all. I am standing behind you in this. No one will ever know. It will be our best-kept secret. Only you and I need ever know the truth!

Unfortunately, we hear too often of Christians, whether working for the church or the government, who embezzle or misappropriate funds. It seems that we forget that God sees all things, despite the evidence from his word. "Does he who implanted the ear not hear? Does he who formed the eye not see? (Ps. 94:9) "The eyes of the

LORD are everywhere, keeping watch on the wicked and the good." (Prov. 15:3)

A liar

"Peter asked her, 'Tell me, is this the price you and Ananias got for the land?' 'Yes,' she said, 'that is the price.' " (Acts 5:8)

Sapphira lied about the amount of money that she and her husband had donated to the church. In our churches, many make public promises and pledges that they will give certain amounts to the church. Many months and years pass and those pledges and promises remain unredeemed. Is it not the same thing as what Ananias and Sapphira did? Ananias and Sapphira

> . . . were not so much misers as thieves and–above all-liars. They wanted the credit and the prestige for sacrificial generosity, without the inconvenience of it. So in order to gain a reputation to which they had no right, they told a brazen lie.[85]

Peter makes clear to Ananias and Sapphira that they are not just telling lies to men but to the Holy Spirit, to God himself. This highlights the fact that our dealings with men are not separate from our relationship with God. If we love God, we should demonstrate that in our relationships with one another. When we lie to another person, we are lying to God. It is a serious thing. We should fear God, who can throw us into hell. We need to be careful not to play games with God, for nothing can be hidden from his sight.

Satan is the father of lies. He is the one who fills our hearts with lies, while the Holy Spirit fills our hearts with truth. Those who speak and practise the truth show that they belong to Jesus, the source of all truth.

A woman who had lost her reverence for God

Sapphira no longer held God in awe and fear. Even though she was in the early days of faith, somehow she thought little of the might and power of the One she had put her trust in.

> Therefore, since we are receiving a kingdom that cannot be shaken let us be thankful and so worship God acceptably with reverence and awe, for our God is a consuming fire. (Heb. 12:28)

A hypocrite

A hypocrite is a play actor. The word describes someone who pretends to be something that he or she is not.[86] Jesus accused the Pharisees of being hypocrites. They were not quite what they seemed. They appeared to be righteous people, but their hearts were far from God. They sought the approval and admiration of men and stood on street corners praying in order to be noticed by the people. They walked through the market in flowing robes, looking for the people's admiration and applause. They put on false appearances of piety. They cleaned the outside of the cup, but the inside was dirty. They were like whitewashed tombs that is, clean on the outside, but full of dead men's bones. (Matt. 23:27) Ananias and Sapphira were not quite what they seemed either. Though they were believers in the early church, they had played the role of hypocrites, and had been 'found wanting.'

> A penetrating question lingers in our minds after we have drawn the curtain on the life of Ananias and Sapphira. Which is really more important to us—to maintain the appearance of spirituality, or genuinely to be what God wants us to be?[87]

Unable to live up to her name

Sapphira means 'beautiful,' but Sapphira failed to live up to her name. Holiness is linked with beauty. To be holy is to be set apart for God. As we grow in holiness, the fruits of the Spirit should be seen in us. (Gal. 5:22-23) Unfortunately, Sapphira failed to display the beauty of holiness.

Forced to endure the consequences for her sin

"At that moment she fell down at his feet and died." (Acts 5:10)

Sometimes, we think that because our God is a forgiving God, (which he undoubtedly is) we will not face any consequences for sins committed. That is not so! Moses sinned and faced the consequence of not being able to enter into the Promised Land. Sapphira's life was taken from her, because of her sin. It does not mean that she was not saved, but God deemed it better to remove her from this visible world. Discipline is part of God's love. It may have been that God wanted this young church to understand his holiness and it certainly had that effect on them. "Great fear seized the whole church and all who heard about these events." (Acts 5:11) Ananias and Sapphira became role models for how not to behave as members of the newly growing community of believers. *"Just as man and wife were united in their conspiracy, so they were united in the judgement that came upon them."*[88]

What lessons can we learn about God?

God is:

A Holy God

"But just as he who called you is holy, so be holy in all you do; for it is written: 'Be holy, because I am holy.'" (1 Pet. 1:16) We ought not to treat God glibly or casually. He is a holy and righteous God and he commands his people to be holy too.

A God who knows all things

"O LORD, you have searched my and you know me. You know when I sit and when I rise; you perceive my thoughts from afar." (Ps. 139:1-2) God knows the truth and sees all things, even the secret things of our hearts. He is more concerned with purity of heart, than with outward appearances.

A God who disciplines in love

"Our fathers disciplined us for a little while as they thought best; but God disciplines us for our good." (Heb. 12:10) A loving parent disciplines his child so that the child knows the difference between what acceptable behaviour is and what it is not. The problem with earthly parents is that we sometimes get it wrong, sometimes over-disciplining and sometimes under-disciplining. God always gets it right and it really is for our good.

Special Focus: Christ in the Story of Sapphira

Jesus is the Lord of the church and the one who purges his church. Jesus showed his concern for holiness and purity in the overturning of the tables in the Temple and in chasing away the moneychangers. (John 2:15) In the story of Ananias and Sapphira God is quick to act against unholy practices in the fledgling church.

Jesus teaches us to fear God and not men.

I tell you my friends, do not be afraid of those who kill the body and after that can do no more. But I will show you whom you should fear: Fear him who, after the killing of the body has power to throw you into hell. Yes, I tell you, fear him. (Luke 12:4-5)

Our fear of men should not hinder us from standing with Christ.

Jesus is the Righteous Judge who knows the intent of the hearts of men. Nothing escapes his notice. However, the Good News is that Christ has died for us so that we the guilty ones might go free. We have a God who forgives sins and wipes the slate clean!

For Further Discussion

1. If Sapphira had objected to her husband's suggestion how might this have affected

* (a) her relationship with her husband?

* (b) her relationship with God?

2. In light of the judgement on Ananias and Sapphira, discuss the seriousness of sin in God's sight.

* (a) The true state of our faith can be seen in how we handle our wealth. Discuss.

* (b) How can we honour God with our possessions and wealth?

* (c) Why are messages on the promise of wealth so popular in churches today when the Bible clearly warns of the many dangers associated with wealth? (cf. Matt. 13:22; Mark 10:22; 1 Tim. 6:17; James 5:1-6)

Chapter Ten
Dorcas–A Woman Who Helped Widows

(Ref: Acts 9: 36-43)

Name

Tabitha, also called Dorcas, which means 'gazelle'- an emblem of beauty or loveliness.[89]

Profile

- A native of Joppa, an ancient seaport (modern day Jaffa).

- A dressmaker.

- No mention of a husband or children.

Background

This story takes place in the midst of Peter's travels around the country. Peter had been instrumental in healing Aeneas, a paralytic who lived in Lydda. (Acts 9:32-35)

Joppa was close to Lydda and, when the disciples heard that Peter was there, they sent for him to come to their aid. This happened around A.D. 38.[90]

What lessons can we learn from Dorcas' life?

Dorcas was:

A disciple

"In Joppa there was a disciple named Tabitha (which when translated, is Dorcas)." (Acts 9:36)

Dorcas is described as a disciple, a learner, just like Mary, "who sat at the Lord's feet and listened to his teaching." (Luke 10:39) Mary was commended for choosing wisely. Similarly, Dorcas is to be commended, as "a woman who fears the Lord is to be praised." (Prov. 31:30-31) She was not just a hearer and a believer of God's word, but a woman who put that word into practice.

Kind and charitable

" . . . who was always doing good and helping the poor." (Acts 9:36) "She was full of good works and acts of charity." (ESV)

Dorcas put her faith into action, reaching out to those in need. Dorcas resembled her Master who went around doing good. Paul taught that good deeds are appropriate for "women who profess to worship God." (1 Tim. 2:9-10) Good works are an apt response to the love of God. The proof of Dorcas' salvation is seen in her acts of kindness and not vice versa. She experienced God's love, and in response reached out in love to others.

> Therefore, as we have opportunity, let us do good to all people, especially to those who belong to the family of believers. (Gal. 6:10)

Dorcas was "always doing good" or "full of good works." Being 'full of good works' suggests "there was little room left for self or self-seeking."[91] Marshall describes Dorcas as *"occupied with good works and charitable actions."*[92] It would appear that Dorcas believed her purpose in life was to worship God and to actively relieve the needs of those less fortunate than herself.

Dorcas was especially remembered for her acts of kindness towards the poor and needy. These acts of kindness had become the habit of her life that is, part of her character and daily life. Dorcas reached out in kindness to those around her and refused to turn a blind eye to those in need. Kindness is a fruit of the Spirit (Gal. 5:22) and should be a characteristic of our Christian lives.

> Dorcas reminds us of Cornelius.

> He and his family were devout and God-fearing; he gave generously to those in need and prayed to God regularly. (Acts10:2)

The people amongst whom she lived, spoke well of Dorcas, just as they did of Cornelius.

> The men replied, "We have come from Cornelius the centurion. He is a righteous and God-fearing man, who is respected by all the Jewish people. (Acts 10:22)

Dorcas also had a good reputation and was well respected in her community. She was well known for her good works.

> Respect is something that is earned or won.

> Make it your ambition to lead a quiet life, to mind your own business and to work with your hands, just as we told you, so that your daily life may win the respect of outsiders and so that you will not be dependent on anybody. (1 Thess. 4:11-12)

What do people say about you, because there is no doubt they are saying something? Some people do not care what others think of them, but it is important to maintain a good reputation. Peter advocates,

> Live such good lives among the pagans that, though they accuse you of doing wrong, they may see your good deeds and glorify God on the day he visits us.
> (1 Pet. 2:12)

Good deeds seem to be a significant factor in maintaining a good reputation. It is not about being good, but about doing good. We need to be careful how we live in our communities so that God may be glorified. In Paul's letter to Timothy, overseers and deacons are required to have a good reputation with outsiders. (1 Tim. 3:7) It is very easy to lose our reputation and once lost, it is very difficult to regain. (Prov. 25:10)

A diligent servant

Dorcas had a heart to serve. There is no mention of her profiting from her sewing. In fact, her best customers were widows who could not afford much. Most people serve others for the money or financial gain that they will receive, but not Dorcas. She gave up her precious time and used her talent sacrificially in service and blessing to others. Much time and effort went into the preparation of garments. Just as Jesus came among us as one who served, (Luke 22:7) so Dorcas, lived in her community as one who served.

Dorcas was not given to idleness. She was a busy, helpful person. Sometimes it can be a problem to find a good worker. Employers can be disappointed at times, that someone whom they employed has turned out to be a lazy person. The person employed to be a help, now becomes a burden. There are many verses in Scripture that speak against laziness. "If a man is lazy, the rafters sag; if his hands are idle, the house leaks." (Eccles. 10:18) "Lazy hands make a man poor, but diligent hands bring wealth." (Prov. 10:4)

> God is not unjust; he will not forget your work and the love you have shown him as you have helped his people and continue to help them. We want each of you to show the same diligence to the very end, in order to make your hope sure. We do not want you to become lazy, but to imitate those who through faith and patience inherit what has been promised. (Heb. 6:10-12)

Dorcas was a lady with a servant heart, and she did it with all the strength that God provided.

> . . . If anyone serves, he should do it with the
> strength God provides, so that in all things God
> may be praised through Jesus Christ. (1 Pet. 4:11)

Surely, she would hear from her Lord "Well done, good and faithful servant!" (Matt. 25:21)

Gifted and Loving

Dorcas was gifted or talented with creativity and skilled in sewing. God gave this woman the ability to sew robes and other clothing for people. Dorcas combined both talent and diligence to produce quality clothes for the people of her community. *"Love generally puts on its work clothes and rolls up its sleeves."*[93]

Dorcas used her hands to demonstrate God's love. She produced garments and gave them to those in need, responding compassionately to their poverty. She was an ordinary woman doing ordinary things but God used her in extraordinary ways. She had eyes to see the people's needs and hands to meet those needs. She did not just think and talk about doing good, but she got up and did it.

We need to look at ourselves and discern the gifts that God has given us and use them for the benefit of others. First, ask God to show you the gift that he has given you. Also, ask yourself the following questions.

What is it that you enjoy doing?

What is it that burdens your heart or deeply concerns you?

As you answer these questions, you may discover the particular gift that God has given you. A gift is given for the benefit of others. Dorcas used hers. Will you use yours?

Helpful to widows

> . . . All the widows stood around him, crying and showing him the robes and other clothing that Dorcas had made while she was still with them. (Acts 9:39)

God is particularly concerned about widows and orphans.

> Religion that God our Father accepts as pure and faultless is this: to look after orphans and widows in their distress and to keep oneself from being polluted by the world. (James 1:27)

HIV/AIDS is an immense problem in Africa and as a result many women are being left as widows and children are being left as orphans. The Christian community is required to show love and concern for the weak, vulnerable, and oppressed members of our society. Many take advantage of these ones, so we need to ensure they find justice. This is real service when we give to help those who cannot do anything to repay us. The fire of AIDS raging all around the world gives Christians and the Church a unique opportunity to minister in Christ's name. It is a chance for us all to teach those around us how vital God's truth is for their lives. It is also a wonderful chance for us to demonstrate the love of Christ to the many who are in darkness and without any earthly hope. God's grace reaches to them. We must be the hands of Christ demonstrating that grace. When we are serving suffering people, we are serving him.94

Dorcas ministered to those who had lost the care of their husbands and breadwinners. Widows, faced with a hopeless future, received care and attention from this compassionate disciple of Jesus.

> Widows, by definition, are poor, on the bottom rung of society, without anyone to represent them or protect them. These are the ones to whom Tabitha, the Gazelle has given life.95

A good example

Dorcas set a great example in how we should daily live our lives in service to others. In her approach to life, she was outward looking and was little concerned about herself. She observed others very well and recognised situations of need. Then she set her mind and hands to work in meeting that need. She put her faith into action, helping those needy ones that came across her path. She was a 'living sacrifice.'

> Therefore, I urge you, brothers in view of God's mercy to offer your bodies as living sacrifices, holy and pleasing to God–this is your spiritual act of worship. (Rom. 12:1)

Just like the woman of noble character, Dorcas had given her heart fully to God and fully in service to mankind. "She opens her arms to the poor and extends her hands to the needy." (Prov. 31:20)

Dead

"About that time, she became sick and died, and her body was washed and placed in an upstairs room." (Acts 9:37)

It would appear that from her friends' reaction to her death, that Dorcas was a big loss to them and to their community. However, even though faced with her death, her friends were not prepared to let her go just yet. Kalas proposes that Dorcas was *"a human being whose impress on others was so great that they simply couldn't let her go."*[96]

Dorcas' friends prepared the body for burial and placed her in an upper room. Marshall regards this action as a demonstration of *"sufficient faith in the possibility of resurrection."*[97] Two men went in search of Peter. On finding him, they pleaded with him not to hesitate but to come to their aid. Dorcas had persevering and persistent friends who were concerned to do all in their power to ensure life for Dorcas. They were not giving up, in spite of the reality of a dead corpse in front of them. Faith is believing without seeing and these friends had it. They were prepared to do everything possible for Dorcas, who had done so much for them.

You have probably heard the expression *"If you want a friend, be a friend."* It would seem that over the years Dorcas had built good friendships. Her friends showed that they were friends indeed at a time when Dorcas was unable to help herself. (See Luke 5:17-26) The kind of friends you keep says a lot about you. "He who walks with the wise grows wise, but a companion of fools suffers harm." (Prov. 13:20) It is good to spend time with the people you want to resemble, because you will grow to resemble the people you spend time with!

When you die, will you be missed as Dorcas was? The Christian community in Joppa grieved at the loss of their friend and did not want to let her go. Her life had affected many and they all mourned her loss and gathered to say what they thought were their final farewells.

However, there was one last thing that could be tried. The faith of her friends was strong enough for one last effort. God could still do something, so they sent for Peter.

Raised to life

Peter followed these disciples to see this amazing woman whom there is no doubt they had already talked to him about. He sees the depth of mourning and sees the evidence of Dorcas' life of good works, and he is moved to act.

> Peter sent them all out of the room; then he got
> down on his knees and prayed. Turning toward the
> dead woman, he said, 'Tabitha, get up.' She opened
> her eyes and seeing Peter got up. He took her by the

> hand and helped her to her feet. Then he called the
> believers and the widows and presented her to them
> alive. (Acts 9: 40- 41)

God can use bad experiences in our lives to bring glory to his name. One prime example of this is the man who had been blind since birth.

> Neither this man nor his parents sinned," said Jesus,
> "but this happened so that the work of God might
> be displayed in his life. (John 9:3)

Dorcas' premature death was not because of sin, but so that the work of God might be displayed in her life. She had extended her own hands to the needy, now the Saviour's hands of healing were extended to her. Dorcas was raised to life and as a result, many put their trust in God. "This became known all over Joppa, and many people believed in the Lord." (Acts 9:42) As Stott declares, *"people heard the word, saw the signs and believed."*[98] I agree with Williams who professes that *"there is nothing wrong with a faith engendered by miracles as long as it leads to a faith that rests on Jesus."*[99]

Miracles do happen and we still need to hold on to the possibility that God can intervene at the last minute, to his praise and glory. God can raise people from the dead. We need to believe, that he can, remembering that he is the sovereign Lord and the final decision of life lies with him.

What lessons can we learn about God?

God is:

A God of impossibilities

"Jesus looked at them and said, "With man this is impossible, but with God all things are possible." (Matt. 19:26) God can do everything. In fact, he delights to do what appears to be impossible, so that He can demonstrate that he truly is God. He is able to raise people from the dead. Even when people are beyond human help, there is still someone who can help. Even in the event of serious illness, God can extend lives. (2 Kings 20: 6)

A defender of widows and orphans

"He defends the cause of the fatherless and the widow, and loves the alien, giving him food and clothing." (Deut. 10:18) As God loves and takes care of the widow and orphan, we his children ought also to be concerned to meet the needs of widows and orphans.

Compassionate

> Even though I walk through the valley of the shadow of death, I will fear no evil, for you are with me; your rod and your staff, they comfort me. (Ps. 23:4)

God's heart was moved to action because of the sadness of the widows at the loss of Dorcas. God saw their need and restored her to them, while at the same time restored hope to their hearts. God feels our pain and weeps with us in times of sorrow and grief. God's miracles demonstrate his compassion and are performed to alleviate human distress and not for providing entertainment.

A wise giver of gifts and talents

> Now to each one the manifestation of the Spirit is given for the common good. To one there is given through the Spirit the message of wisdom, to another the message of knowledge. . . . All these are the work of one and the same Spirit, and he gives them to each one, just as he determines. (1 Cor. 12:7-11)

Each of us are given gifts for the building up of the body of Christ. Each of us has our own unique gifting, which is to be used to serve others. God makes no mistakes and gives gifts as he chooses and as he knows are best for us and for others.

Special Focus: Christ in the Story of Dorcas

Jesus is the compassionate one, moved by the infirmities of his people. Through Peter his disciple, God raised Dorcas back to life. The miracle of resurrection resulted in people putting their trust in the Lord.

Dorcas was raised in this instance, but she would later die as all men would. Jesus was raised and lives for evermore.

> I am the resurrection and the life. He who believes in me will live, even though he dies; and whoever lives and believes in me will never die . . . (John 11:25-26)

Jesus' resurrection assures us that we will also be raised and will live with him for evermore.

> But Christ has indeed been raised from the dead, the first fruits of those who have fallen asleep . . . For as in Adam all die, so in Christ all will be made alive. (1 Cor. 15:20-22)

We will live and so will Dorcas, for evermore!

For Further Discussion

1. Peter prayed and God raised Dorcas from the dead! Can such miracles happen today?

2. Think about practical ways in which you can show care and compassion to those in need. (See Matt. 25:31-40)

3. Like Dorcas, how can you use your profession to benefit others and glorify God?

Chapter Eleven
Lydia – A Woman Who Sought God

(Ref: Acts 16:11-15)

Name

Lydia may refer to the town where she came from, that is. the lady from Lydia.[100] 'Lydia' means 'bending'[101] and is apt in light of Lydia's compliant response to the gospel.

Profile

- Originally from Thyatira in Asia, famous for purple dyes.

- A dealer in purple cloth.

- Lived and worked in Philippi (a Roman colony) in Greece.

- May have been a single businesswoman.

Background

Following Paul's vision of a man of Macedonia

> standing and begging him to come and help, Paul
> and his companions concluded that God wanted
> them to preach the gospel in Macedonia. In
> response, they set out from Troas and travelled as
> far as Philippi where this special meeting with
> Lydia took place. (Acts 16: 6-12)

These events took place at the beginning of Paul's second missionary journey around A.D. 50.[102]

What lessons can we learn from Lydia's life?

Lydia was:

A woman of prayer and a worshipper of God

> On the Sabbath we went outside the city gate to the
> river, where we expected to find a place of prayer.
> We sat down and spoke to the women who had
> gathered there. (Acts 16:13)

The first mention made of Lydia is concerning prayer. Lydia is found amongst a group of women praying outside the city gates. It appears that there was no synagogue in Philippi possibly because there were not enough men to make up the required quorum of ten. Therefore, in the absence of a synagogue, Lydia and other women met together beside the river to pray. It was Paul's custom or strategy that whenever he entered a new area, he first sought out the local synagogue. He found these Jewish places of worship a useful platform for the proclamation of the gospel. In this case, there was no synagogue, so Paul headed for the most likely place of prayer, that is, by the river, where ritual washing could take place.

Not only was Lydia involved in prayer, but also, she is described as "a worshipper of God." (v.14) This phrase may suggest that Lydia was not always a Jew. Stott states that she was *"believing and behaving like a Jew without having become one."*[103] She may have been a God-fearer that is, a Gentile who worshipped the God of Israel but had not become an actual Jew. Cornelius is another example of a God fearer.

> At Caesarea there was a man named Cornelius, a centurion in what was known as the Italian Regiment. He and all his family were devout and God-fearing. (Acts 10:1-2)

Lydia, like Cornelius was a faithful worshipper of God as far as her knowledge of him went.

> As an unmarried Gentile woman, she was unable by the laws of Judaism to convert. Obviously, she was

a convert in her heart, but an outsider by the structures of the institution.[104]

Lydia knew there was a God and worshipped in the only way she knew how. However, God had ordained it that this seeker of God would meet his messenger on this particular day. Little did she know that God had decided that this ordinary day was going to become an extraordinary day! This day her relationship with God would become real and her life would be changed forever.

A listener, eager to learn

"One of those listening was a woman named Lydia." (Acts 16:14)

God directed Paul, through a dream, to go to this area to preach the gospel.

> During the night Paul had a vision of a man of Macedonia standing and begging him, 'Come over to Macedonia and help us.' (Acts 16:9)

Paul, Timothy, and Silas had gone in response to God's instruction and here by the river, outside the city of Philippi, Paul and his companions found a group of ladies eager to listen to their message.

A Macedonian male may have been the first to call for Paul's gospel (16:9) but Macedonian women are the first to hear and receive it.[105]

Lydia especially was happy to hear Paul. She was not only eager to allow these men the opportunity to speak to her and the other women, but God had prepared her heart to hear this very message. Lydia had longed to know God more intimately and as she listened, she knew that she had found what she was looking for. She had sought God and had found him. "You will seek me and find me when you seek me with all your heart." (Jer. 29:12)

Paul, in his own words, was not an eloquent speaker so of himself he could not have persuaded anyone to believe in God. When Paul wrote to the Corinthians he says,

When I came to you, brothers, I did not come with eloquence or superior wisdom as I proclaimed to you the testimony about God. For I resolved to know nothing while I was with you except Jesus Christ and him crucified. I came to you in weakness and fear, and with much trembling. My message and my preaching were not with wise and persuasive words, but with a demonstration of the

Spirit's power, so that your faith might not rest on
men's wisdom, but on God's power. (1 Cor. 2:1-5)

Paul claimed no glory for himself. Paul knew that
conversion was the work of God alone, but God at the
same time chose to use an imperfect vessel like Paul to
bring his message to those who needed to hear. Lydia
listened to Paul speaking and her heart was touched by
what she heard. God continues to use imperfect vessels
like us to share the gospel with others, to introduce Jesus to
others. He also continues to prepare hearts to hear his
word.

Open to God

"The Lord opened her (Lydia's) heart to respond to Paul's
message." (Acts 16:14)

The work of salvation is God's work alone. "No one
can come to me unless the Father who sent me draws him .
. ." (John 6:44) God alone enables believers to heed his
message of salvation and God stirred this woman to
respond to him.

Her conversion is attributed to the fact that the Lord
opened her heart, and this set the seal on the
obedience of the missionaries in crossing over to
Macedonia at his bidding.[106]

Paul spoke, Lydia listened, and the Spirit of God opened her heart. This was the work of God in her life. Many hearts lie cold and hard, but Lydia's was soft and pliable and she did not resist God's call to believe. "As she listened with intensity to what was being said, the Master gave her a trusting heart–and she believed." (MSG) "The Lord opened her heart to pay attention to what was said by Paul." (ESV) She was quick to listen and quick to respond. There was no hesitancy here. She responded in faith. She knew deep within her heart that all Paul said was true.

Many people hear and know that what they hear is true, but they delay making any decision. They put off wholeheartedly following Jesus, believing perhaps that there will be time for commitment later on in life. Perhaps they feel that a commitment to Christ might be somehow inconvenient for the moment. Unfortunately, many put it off until it is too late. Dear brothers and sisters, learn from Lydia, a wise woman who responded to the gospel with no hesitancy.

In the right place at the right time

Philippi was the right place, and this was the right time. Lydia had the right heart and the right response to the message. The Holy Spirit guided Paul not only to Philippi, but also specifically to Lydia. Paul had not planned to visit Philippi but God was the director of his path and in his providence brought Paul into contact with this woman. This insignificant woman led to a rich harvest of believers. She is the first recorded convert of Paul's in Europe and subsequently her home became the place where the first church was established in Europe.

Through Lydia a door for the gospel and the expansion of the Christian church was opened into Europe. She was a key instrument in the hand of God. Lydia was impacted by the gospel and in turn influenced its spread further afield; much like the woman at the well in John 4 who was instrumental in the spreading of faith to her community. Because of her encounter with Christ, the word of God spread. It is clear from these examples, that the faith of one person can make a difference and can have far-reaching effects.

A wealthy businesswoman

" . . . a dealer in purple cloth from the city of Thyatira." (Acts 16:14)

Lydia traded in purple cloth, which was expensive and was often worn by royalty or those of the nobility. It appears that she was a wealthy businesswoman as she had a house big enough to offer Paul and his companions a place to lay their heads. The Bible also speaks of her household, so she had others living with her, so there is no doubt that she was a woman of means. Despite being a woman, she had become successful in business. Kalas advocates that

> . . . she had to have been a very strong person. Not only was the business world dominated by men but also Lydia came from another region, which made an extra burden to prove herself . . . [107]

Yet, despite the disadvantages of gender and culture, Lydia had made it in a male domain.

Many women are involved in business or trading in Africa. Many work tirelessly, night and day just to make ends meet and often there can be a temptation to cut corners in order to enrich oneself. Nevertheless, our relationship with God should affect how we do business. Remember to put God first, in whatever business you are involved! Amos condemns those in business whose business practices are less than ethical.

> You can't wait for the Sabbath day to be over and the religious festivals to end so you can get back to cheating the helpless. You measure out grain with dishonest measures and cheat the buyer with dishonest scales. (Amos 8:5 NLT)

God is not just a Sunday God, but an everyday of the week God, who is concerned about ethical business practices.

Some people suggest that Christianity is for those who are down on their luck and need a crutch, something to hold them up. Lydia needed no crutch, as she was a successful and wealthy woman. Christianity is open to all, both the rich and the poor. God

> . . . wants all men to be saved and to come to a knowledge of the truth. For there is one God and one mediator between God and men, the man Christ Jesus who gave himself as a ransom for all men . . . (1 Tim. 2:4-5).

God desires that all people be saved whatever their station in life, whether they are rich or poor, or whatever position they hold in life, whether it be a high one or a low one. The truth is that we all need God. The Good News of salvation in Christ thrilled Lydia. She responded gladly to the Lord's offer of love and mercy. *"For all her evident social accomplishment, she had a spiritual need satisfied by hearing God's word."*[108]

Baptized

" . . . she and the members of her household were baptized." (Acts 16:15)

Lydia, having heard, and responded to the gospel wanted to show her public identification with Christ. Along with her household, she identified with Christ in his death and resurrection in the public act of baptism. They went down into the waters of death and rose to new life in Christ. Her whole household was baptised indicating that Lydia's home was now a Christian home. Just as Cornelius and his household were baptised so was Lydia, and all those who lived with her.

A woman of hospitality

> When she and the members of her household were baptized, she invited us to her home. 'If you consider me a believer in the Lord,' she said, 'come and stay at my house' And she persuaded us. (Acts 16:15)

Lydia's newfound Christian faith moved into action immediately. Her open heart led automatically to an open house. Immediately she invited Paul and his companions to stay in her home. This was no half-hearted gesture from Lydia. She was not merely asking out of politeness or because she ought to, but Lydia really wanted these men of God to stay at her home. She was so thrilled by their message that she desired their very presence in her home. Perhaps there she would have an opportunity not only to hear more but also to enjoy the presence of God that surrounded these faithful messengers.

She was honoured that these special messengers from God should stay at her home. They had brought her the greatest message that she had ever heard and there is no doubt she wanted to enjoy their company for longer. Lydia would not take no for an answer, so Paul and his companions remained with her for a time. Through opening her house to Paul and his companions, she also provided them with protection being strangers in a foreign land.

The Spirit of God was living and active in Lydia. She had a servant heart and was eager to give back. Hospitality is very much a part of the African way of life and it is especially a part of the Christian life.

> Do not forget to entertain strangers, for by so doing some people have entertained angels without knowing it. (Heb. 13:2)

(See Chapter Twelve: Priscilla)

Lydia was concerned that the needs of these messengers of God be met. It is clear that Paul and his companions had felt quite at home here, as after being released from prison it is to Lydia that they first go.

> After Paul and Silas came out of prison, they went to Lydia's house, where they met with the brothers and encouraged them. (Acts 16:40)

Lydia's home became a meeting place for the growing church in that area. There is no doubt that Lydia became part of the nucleus of the new church that was established as a result of numerous conversions in Philippi, for example the slave girl and the jailer and his family. (Acts 16:16-34)

A generous and kind woman

Lydia did not have to be taught to be generous. Having discovered God's love, she opened her heart to love others with her wealth. (see also Luke 19:8) God's presence changes our perspective on wealth. Lydia was aware that her resources had come from God and were to be used to bless others. It seems that the church that was established in the area of Philippi continued in the same spirit of generosity. Later Paul spoke kindly of their abundant gift.

> And now, brothers, we want you to know about the grace that God has given the Macedonian churches. Out of the most severe trial, their overflowing joy and extreme poverty welled up in rich generosity. For I testify that they gave as much as they were able, and even beyond their ability . . . (2 Cor. 8: 1-5)

Paul in his message to the Philippian' church describes them as his 'joy and crown.' (Rom. 4:1) Lydia gave herself firstly to God and then gave herself in love to others.

Single

Lydia does not appear to be married and for those who are single she is a good role model. In Africa, it is generally expected that a woman will marry. It is important to know that to marry is good and not to marry is also good. Paul says,

> . . . the unmarried or betrothed woman is anxious about the things of the Lord, how to be holy in body and spirit. But the married woman is anxious about worldly things, how to please her husband. I say this for your own benefit, not to lay any restraint on you, but to promote good order and to secure your undivided devotion to the Lord. (1 Cor. 7:34-35 ESV)

God can use both married people and single people. As God's devoted servants, we should not allow ourselves to be pushed or compelled into marriage but should carefully and prayerfully decide what is best in our own case.

A woman of courage

Lydia demonstrated courage in opening her home to this group of Christians despite the fact that there might have been repercussions because of her association with Christianity.

> The followers of Jesus represented a small religious movement that was suspect in almost every quarter. It was daring enough just to identify yourself as being sympathetic with such a marginal body; Lydia chose to make her home their headquarters.[109]

Lydia took risks that might have endangered her life and her livelihood. However, she feared God more than man and was prepared to stand on the side of truth. She had found the most precious thing and nothing else mattered and her home became a centre for Christian outreach into Europe. Have you found this priceless treasure? I pray that you would open your heart as Lydia did and respond to God's gift of salvation in Christ.

What lessons can we learn about God?

God is:

One who sends messengers with his message of salvation

Lydia was ready to hear the gospel, but someone had to go and share the message with her. Paul was God's chosen instrument.

How, then, can they call on the one they have not believed in? And how can they believe in the one of whom they have not heard? And how can they hear without someone preaching to them? And how can they preach unless they are sent? As it is written, 'How beautiful are the feet of those who bring good news!' (Rom. 10:14-15)

Sovereign

God is in control, and he is working out his purposes. He engineers circumstances and orchestrates apparent chance happenings. Because he knows what he is doing, we can trust him. *"Our task is to preach the Word in the power of the Holy Spirit and leave the results to him."*[110]

A lover of all people

God's message of salvation is for all. It is God's desire that all men be saved. Not all men will be saved, but that is not God's fault. When presented with the gospel we have a choice to believe or not to.

An extraordinary God who can turn an ordinary day into an extraordinary one

God answers prayers. One day our prayer seems far from answered and the next day unexpectedly, the answer comes. As Lydia sought God with all her heart, her prayer was answered the day that Paul showed up.

Special Focus: Christ in the Story of Lydia

Lydia, though a wealthy woman and influential businesswoman, shows the humility of a servant. Just like her Master, she was willing to serve others. Christ is the greatest example of humility and servanthood.

> Your attitude should be the same as that of Christ Jesus: Who, being in very nature God, did not consider equality with God something to be grasped, but made himself nothing, taking the very nature of a servant, being found in human likeness. And being found in appearance as a man, he humbled himself and became obedient to death–even death on a cross! (Phil. 2:5-8)

"For even the Son of Man did not come to be served, but to serve, and to give his life as a ransom for many." (Mark 10:45) Christ gave up his life so that we might live.

From heaven you came helpless babe,

entered our world, your glory veiled,

Not to be served but to serve,

and give your life that we might live.

So let us learn how to serve

and in our lives enthrone Him,

Each other's needs to prefer,

for it is Christ we're serving.[111]

For Further Discussion

1. Discuss the importance of hospitality in Christian ministry.

2. What is the significance of baptism for believers?

3. "Now to the unmarried and the widows I say: it is good for them to stay unmarried, as I am." (1 Cor. 7:1) Discuss the advantages and disadvantages of serving God as a single person.

Chapter Twelve
Priscilla – A Woman Who Taught the Truth

(Ref: Acts. 18-19; Rom. 16:3-4; 1 Cor. 16:19; 2 Tim. 4:19)

Name

Priscilla or Prisca means original, worthy or venerable.[112]

Profile

- Married to Aquila.

- Worked together with her husband as a team.

- A Bible teacher and a tent maker.

- May have been a native of Pontus (like her husband). Lived in Rome, Corinth and Ephesus.

- No mention of children.

Background

Paul had spent some time in Athens where he made his

famous speech to the people of Athens in which he revealed to them the unknown God. (Acts 17:16-34) Following his time in Athens Paul travelled to Corinth where he met Aquila and his wife Priscilla. These events took place during Paul's second missionary journey between A.D. 50 and A.D. 52. [113]

What lessons can we learn from Priscilla's life?

Priscilla was:

A persecuted believer

> After this, Paul left Athens and went to Corinth. There he met a Jew named Aquila, a native of Pontus, who had recently come from Italy with his wife Priscilla because Claudius had ordered all the Jews to leave Rome. (Acts 18:1-3)

Priscilla and Aquila were on the move. They had recently come from Rome, having faced expulsion at the hands of the emperor Claudius. This couple were victims of religious oppression at the hands of the Roman emperor, but what had seemed a trying and difficult experience in their lives had worked for the good of the kingdom of God. Priscilla and Aquila had set up home in Corinth and had continued to work for the glory of God. It is here in Corinth that Paul meets this couple for the first time. (No mention is made of their conversion so it would seem that they had become Christians before arriving in Corinth.) Paul had come alone to Corinth without his companions Silas and Timothy, however God blessed him "with the acquaintance of Aquila and Priscilla."[114]

Paul knew the importance of Corinth as a commercial centre. *"If trade could radiate from Corinth in all directions, so could the gospel."*[115] Paul must surely have recognised God's hand at work in the transfer of Priscilla and Aquila to Corinth, to support his ministry, at the right time. If Paul arrived in Corinth as a *"discouraged man"* as suggested by Fernando, then the provision of Aquila and Priscilla was just the encouragement Paul needed.[116]

A co-worker with Paul

"Greet Priscilla and Aquila, my fellow workers in Christ Jesus." (Rom. 16:3)

Paul commends this husband-and-wife team and has no qualms about honouring this lady as a fellow-worker, one who worked hard for the sake of the gospel. Priscilla was no slacker but worked tirelessly to establish the church of God. This couple did not just watch Paul at work, they were also active workers alongside him. Like Paul, this couple were motivated by the same goal, that is, the proclamation of the gospel and the growth of the church. Priscilla and Aquila helped Paul in the ministry, working alongside him on many occasions and Paul acknowledged them as his equals. The noted apostle Paul was not the big man in ministry but was happy to associate himself with others who worked hard to serve the Lord. Too often within the church, we see too much striving for position and not enough co-labouring. In serving God, we are not rivals but co-labourers. Let us work together to see God's kingdom established. "Be devoted to one another in brotherly love. Honour one another above yourselves." (Rom. 12:10)

A courageous and loyal friend to Paul

Paul speaks of this couple with great fondness and admiration. In his ministry he had faced the experience of being let down by friends and co-workers, but this special couple had never let him down. Paul saw them as loyal and faithful friends. We all need friends, and Paul found what he needed in Aquila and Priscilla. They proved to be trustworthy colleagues on whom Paul could depend. They were a great support to Paul in the tough task of Christian ministry.

Paul declares that Aquila and Priscilla "risked their lives for me" (Rom. 16:3), or "risked their necks for my life." (ESV) Literally, this couple had put their lives on the line for Paul's sake. They were sacrificial in their service to Paul, putting Paul's security above their own. Somehow, somewhere, this couple put Paul's well-being before their own interests and in the process had put their own lives at risk. In doing so, they had not only won Paul's respect and thankfulness, but also that of the churches of the Gentiles. (Rom. 16:3)

A tentmaker

"Paul went to see them and because he was a tentmaker as they were he stayed and worked with them." (Acts 18:2b–3)

Priscilla and Aquila had been trained in a trade that they could fall back on in order to provide an income for themselves. It is possible that they learned this as children because most Jewish parents would have felt it was a vital part of a child's training to learn a particular trade. Thus,

Joseph had trained Jesus to be a carpenter. Priscilla and Aquila made tents together and were not afraid of hard work. Laziness was far from them. They were a self-supporting couple.

There is a time for everything. Paul at times received gifts towards his ministry and depended on others for support while at other times, he worked to support himself. At this particular time, Paul joined this couple to work with his hands to provide for his own needs. Paul later in his message to the Thessalonians encouraged this work ethic.

> "Make it your ambition to lead a quiet life, to mind your own business and to work with your hands, just as we told you, so that your daily life may win the respect of outsiders and so that you will not be dependent on anybody." (1 Thess. 4:11)

"For even when we were with you, we gave you this rule: If a man will not work, he shall not eat." (2 Thess. 3:10) The Scriptures generally encourage diligent labour and admonish laziness. "A sluggard does not plough in season so at harvest time he looks but finds nothing." (Prov. 20:4; see also Prov. 6: 6-11)

'Tentmaking' is a term used within mission today.

> The expression describes cross-cultural messengers
> of the gospel, who support themselves by their own
> professional or business expertise, while at the same
> time being involved in mission.[117]

Sometimes the best way to reach others is to work alongside them and use the particular skills that God has given us, for his glory.

A hospitable hostess

Despite the stress of the recent moves from their home in Rome, Priscilla's heart and home were open to visitors. Priscilla and her husband were happy to follow the custom of Middle Eastern hospitality to strangers, so on meeting Paul, a stranger for the first time, Priscilla opened her home to him. As a result, a lifelong friendship developed between this couple and Paul. They were like-minded believers travelling on the same road of pilgrimage.

Not only that, but Priscilla was content to put up with the inconvenience of a church meeting in their home. "Greet also the church that meets at their house." (Rom. 16:5) " . . . Aquila and Priscilla greet you warmly in the Lord and so does the church that meets at their house." (1

Cor. 16:19) Priscilla had to sacrifice personal comfort and the privacy of her own home to cater for the growing church. There is no doubt that the church met often to pray together and listen to the preaching and teaching of God's word. This was a disturbance of privacy that Priscilla was happy to put up with, for the greater good.

Jesus had demonstrated hospitality in his own ministry at various times for example, the feeding of the 5,000 (Matt. 14: 13-21; Mark 6:30-44) and Aquila and Priscilla had followed in their Master's ways. "Share with God's people who are in need. Practise hospitality." (Rom. 12:13) God, through Paul's words encourages the Christian practice of hospitality. It is not just hospitality to those we know.

> While hospitality can include acts of welcoming family and friends, its meaning within the Christian biblical and historical traditions has focused on receiving the alien and extending one's resources to them.[118]

> Hospitality is more than an action. It is more even than a state of mind that we generate now and then for our convenience. It is a particular way of looking at the world. In its simplest form, hospitality is seeing the stranger through the eyes of Jesus. It is

> choosing to look for Jesus in the eyes of each
> stranger. It is loving the stranger. [119]

A travelling companion to Paul

> Paul stayed on in Corinth for some time. Then he
> left the brothers and sailed for Syria, accompanied
> by Priscilla and Aquila . . . They arrived at Ephesus
> where Paul left Priscilla and Aquila. (Acts 18:18-19)

Priscilla and Aquila travelled with Paul on one of his missionary journeys. While Paul continued his travels, Paul left them behind in Ephesus. It would appear that Stott is right in surmising that, *this married couple . . . exemplified an extraordinary degree of mobility.*[120] The fact that they did not have children made it possible for them to move with ease, when required. More than likely, they were able to continue their tentmaking wherever they moved to.

A teacher

> When Priscilla and Aquila heard him they invited
> him to their home and explained to him the way of
> God more adequately. (Acts 18: 26)

It was while they were there at Ephesus that a Jew named Apollos came to Ephesus and spoke fervently about Jesus. As Priscilla and Aquila listened, they noted that something was missing from what he said and needed to be corrected. Priscilla appears to have been a competent, able teacher. Along with her husband, she set about the task of teaching Apollos. This was no easy task as Apollos was described as "a learned man, with a thorough knowledge of the Scriptures." (Acts 18:24) Still Apollos had something to learn from this woman of wisdom.

This couple taught with grace. They did not embarrass Apollos but took him aside to their home, also the meeting place of the church, to educate him further. They were able to add the missing piece to Apollos' knowledge. It is clear that they saw the potential in this young preacher to influence others and it was important that his message be accurate. He was such a gifted speaker that he needed to be corrected because his influence would go far. This couple were concerned with the truth and could not ignore the incompleteness of Apollos' message. Apollos took no offense at their teaching but moved on to other places now better equipped to preach the truth about Christ.

> When Apollos wanted to go to Achaia, the brothers
> encouraged him and wrote to the disciples there to
> welcome him. On arriving, he was a great help to
> those who by grace had believed. For he vigorously
> refuted the Jews in public debate, proving from the
> Scriptures that Jesus was the Christ. (Acts 18:27-28)

It is important to know your calling. God does not call every man or every woman to be a teacher of God's Word.

> Not many of you should presume to be teachers, my
> brothers, because you know that we who teach will
> be judged more strictly. (James 3:1)

However, maybe God is calling you. It is important to know the ministry to which God has called you.

It is important also to note the necessity of training our daughters. Even in the time of Jesus, women were not encouraged to learn, but Jesus was happy to teach women. Mary is noted for sitting at Jesus' feet listening to his every word. Jesus commended her choice. "Mary has chosen what is better, and it will not be taken from her." (Luke 10:38-42) The woman at the well in John 4 is also another example of Jesus' willingness to teach women about the deep things of God. If women are going to be able to function well in society and in the church, they need to learn. (see also 1 Tim. 2:11)

Women need not be intellectual inferiors. It must become outdated to fail to educate our daughters in Africa. Still in some societies, girls in particular, do not receive a basic education.

Girls reap enormous benefits from post-primary education, including skills that translate into employment and empowerment. In addition, there is a correlation between education beyond primary school and having healthier families and lower fertility rates. Yet despite the multiple benefits of secondary education, four out of every five girls in Africa go without it.[121]

Some of the reasons for the low state of education amongst girls include poverty and early marriage to mention a few. If money is limited in a family, then the boy is enrolled at school ahead of the girl in the family. Things have improved more recently, and we welcome these improvements. The education of girls should be high on our list of priorities.

Priscilla could not have been an effective Bible teacher and expounder of God's word, if she had not received a good foundation of basic education.

Part of a team ministry

Aquila and Priscilla appear to have complemented each other, forming an effective team. They were a united couple working together for the furtherance of God's kingdom. In all things, they were together.

Couples can have an effective ministry together. Too many pastors work independently of their wives. Some even feel that their wives would not be of any assistance to them. Mostly the problem lies in the fact that some wives are not adequately versed in the Scriptures, when if trained they could be of tremendous assistance to their husbands. This is sad as often couples can work together effectively.

Priscilla was her husband's complement, his close companion. These two worked together for the extension

> Two are better than one, because they have a return for their work. If one falls down, his friend can help him up. But pity the man who falls and has no one to help him up! Also, if two lie down together, they will keep warm. But how can one keep warm alone? Though one may be overpowered, two can defend themselves. A cord of three strands is not easily broken. (Ecclesiastes 4:9 – 12)

of God's kingdom. Together they preached the truth and built-up believers in the faith. Aquila had truly found his soul mate, a woman willing to cooperate with him–a real gem. "Houses and wealth are inherited from parents, but a prudent wife is from the Lord." (Prov. 19:4) Aquila had been truly blessed as he had been given the perfect partner to assist him in the work of Christian ministry.

Simply by mentioning her name along with her husband's suggests that Priscilla was no back seat Christian but actively involved in the ministry of teaching. There is no point in wasting time arguing about whether Priscilla was the more prominent teacher, because at times her name is mentioned first before that of her husband. What is important is the fact that they worked together well as a team. Together they advanced the kingdom of God wherever they found themselves. Paul certainly trusted them and applauded their ministry. He knew he could rely on them to do a good job.

Joyful

This couple found joy in serving the Lord. They lived full lives. There is no hint of a life of regret over not having children. They were parents of a different kind as nurturers of new believers. They did not divorce over the matter of not having children. Instead, they saw this as an opportunity for more whole-hearted devotion to their God. They were inseparable, sharing the highs and lows of life in service to God together. They had a solid marriage that was unshaken by a lack of children in the home. Priscilla was the right helper for Aquila. (Gen. 2:18)

They supported each other in their calling to serve God. This couple demonstrate what can happen when a husband and wife follow God's instruction and become one.

> Haven't you read, he replied, that at the beginning the Creator made them male and female, and said, For this reason a man will leave his father and mother and be united to his wife and the two will become one flesh? So, they are no longer two, but one. Therefore, what God has joined together, let man not separate. (Matt. 19:4-6)

Aquila and Priscilla walked as one, together wholeheartedly devoted to their Lord. Both were committed to God and to each other.

A woman with many roles to play

Priscilla was called to handle many different roles and she appears to have handled them well. There is no doubt that she must have been gifted in organisation. She was a wife, a tentmaker, a hostess, a church leader, a teacher, a missionary. So how did she do it all? It would appear that she did it in the strength of God and for his glory.

> Therefore, my dear brothers, stand firm. Let nothing move you. Always give yourselves fully to the work of the Lord, because you know that your labour in the Lord is not in vain. (1 Cor. 15:58)

What lessons can we learn about God?

God is:

The giver of gifts for service

> Now to each one the manifestation of the Spirit is given for the common good. To one there is given through the Spirit the message of wisdom, to another the message of knowledge . . . All these are the work of one and the same Spirit, and he gives them to each one, just as he determines. (1 Cor. 12:7-11)

Priscilla was gifted with the special gift of understanding, interpreting and teaching God's word. Her gender was not an obstacle to the ministry of the word of God and was called into the ministry just as her husband Aquila was. Priscilla refused to hide her light under a bushel. Whatever gift God has given you, use it for God's glory.

Able to take care of us wherever we are

"I was young and now I am old, yet I have never seen the righteous forsaken or their children begging bread." (Ps. 37:25) Aquila and Priscilla were constantly on the move and served God faithfully wherever they found themselves. They were flexible and good missionary material, able to cope in whatever situation they found themselves. God took care of them wherever they were, and they blossomed where they were planted.

Special focus: Christ in the story of Priscilla

Priscilla and Aquila took Apollos aside and instructed him further in the way of God in much the same vein as Jesus took his disciples aside and explained things to them.

> He did not say anything to them without using a parable. But when he was alone with his own disciples, he explained everything. (Mark 4:34)

Jesus is the Great Teacher. In the Scriptures Jesus is shown to be different than the teachers of the law, as he taught with authority.

> When Jesus had finished saying these things, the crowds were amazed at his teaching, because he taught as one who had authority, and not as their teachers of the law. (Matt. 7:29)

We can trust Jesus' teachings for he speaks the truth. Wise people heed Christ's instructions and put them into practice.

> Therefore, everyone who hears these words of mine and puts them into practice is like a wise man who built his house on the rock. (Matt. 7:24)

For Further Discussion

1. Think about ways in which your home can be used to facilitate the ministry of God's word.

2. Couples can be effective in ministry together. What are the advantages and disadvantages of such a team ministry?

3. What practical steps do you need to take to become an approved workman who is able to handle the word of truth (2 Tim. 2:15)?

Rise up women of the truth,

Stand and sing to broken hearts,

Who can know the healing power

Of our glorious King of love.

Shout to the north and the south,

Sing to the east and the west:

Jesus is Saviour to all,

Lord of heaven and earth.[122]

Bibliography and Recommended Reading

Bibles

Beers, Ronald A. (Gen. ed.) *Life Application Study Bible: NIV*. Grand Rapids: Zondervan, 1991.

Grudem, Wayne (Gen. ed.) *ESV Study Bible*. Illinois: Crossway, 2008.

Syswerda, Jean (Gen. ed.) *Women of Faith Study Bible: NIV*. Grand Rapids: Zondervan, 2001.

Books

Adeyemo, Tokunboh. *African Bible Commentary*. Grand Rapids: Zondervan, 2006.

Anderson, Allan. *An Introduction to Pentecostalism: Global Charismatic Christianity*. Cambridge: University Press, 2004.

Atkinson, David. *The Message of Ruth*. Leicester: IVP, 1994.

Baldwin, Joyce G. *1 & 2 Samuel*. Leicester: IVP, 1988.

Baldwin, Joyce G. Esther: *An Introduction and Commentary*. Leicester: IVP, 1984.

Bentley, Michael. *Saving a Fallen World*. Darlington: Evangelical Press, 1992.

Bock, Darrell L. *Luke*. Grand Rapids: Zondervan, 1996.

Breneman, Mervin. *The New American Commentary: Ezra, Nehemiah, Esther*. USA: Broadman & Holman, 1993.

Davis, Dale Ralph. *1 Samuel: Looking on the Heart*. Fearn: Christian Focus, 2000.

DeVries, Simon J. *Word Biblical Commentary: 1 Kings*. Waco Texas: Word Books, 1985.

Dunn James J.G. and John W. Rogerson (eds.) *Eerdmans Commentary on the Bible*. Grand Rapids: Eerdmans, 2003.

Evans, Craig A. *Luke*. Massachusetts: Hendrickson Publishers, 1990.

Evans, Mary J. *Women in the Bible*. Cumbria: Paternoster Press, 1983.

Evans, Mary J. *The Message of Samuel*. Nottingham: IVP, 2004.

Fernando, Ajith. *The NIV Application Commentary: Acts*. Grand Rapids: Zondervan, 1998.

Freedman, David Noel. (ed.-in chief) *The Anchor Bible Dictionary Vol. 1*. New York: Doubleday, 1992.

Gaebelein, Frank E. (ed) *The Expositor's Bible Commentary Vol 9*. Grand Rapids: Zondervan, 1984.

Garland, Jean & Dr Mike Blyth. *AIDS is real and it's in our church*. Bukuru: Africa Christian Textbooks, 2005.

Harris, Robert L., Gleason L. Archer, & Bruce K Waltke. *Theological Wordbook of the Old Testament Vol I and II*. Chicago: Moody Press, 1980.

Hershberger, Michele. *A Christian View of Hospitality*. Scottdale: Herald Press, 1999.

Horrobin, Peter & Greg Leavers (comps). *Complete Mission Praise.* London: Harper Collins, 2005.

James, Sharon. *God's Design for Women: Biblical Womanhood for Today.* Darlington: Evangelical Press, 2002.

Kalas, J. Ellsworth. *Strong Was Her Faith: Women of the New Testament.* Nashville: Abingdon Press, 2007.

Keck, Leander E. (ed.) *The New Interpreter's Bible Vol. II.* Nashville: Abingdon Press, 1998.

Keck, Leander E. (ed.) *The New Interpreter's Bible Vol. X.* Nashville: Abingdon Press, 2002.

Keddie, Gordon, J. *Even in Darkness.* Darlington: Evangelical Press, 1985.

Kirk, J. Andrew. *Mission Under Scrutiny: Confronting Current Challenges.* London: Darton, Longman & Todd, 2006.

Klein, Ralph W. *Word Biblical Commentary 10: I Samuel.* Waco, TX: Word Books, 1983.

Marshall, I. Howard. *The Acts of the Apostles: An Introduction and Commentary.* Leicester: IVP, 1999.

McCarter, P. Kyle, Jr. *I Samuel: The Anchor Bible Vol. 8.* New York: Doubleday, 1980.

McGrath, Joanna Collicutt, *Jesus and the Gospel Women.* London: SPCK, 2009.

Meyers, Carol L., Toni Craven & Ross Shepard Kraemer. *Women in Scripture.* Grand Rapids: Eerdmans, 2001.

Moltmann-Wendell, Elisabeth. *The Women Around Jesus*. New York: Crossroad, 1996.

Mounce, William D. (ed.) *Mounce's Complete Expository Dictionary of Old and New Testament* Words. Grand Rapids: Zondervan, 2006.

Neil, William. *The New Century Bible Commentary: The Acts of the Apostles*. Grand Rapids: Eerdmans, 1986.

Oden, Amy G. (ed.) *And You Welcomed Me*. Nashville: Abingdon Press, 2001.

Patterson, Dorothy K. & Rhonda H. Kelley. (eds.) *Women's Evangelical Commentary: New Testament*, Nashville: Broadman & Holman, 2006.

Pierce, Ronald. W., Rebecca M. Groothuis, & Gordon D. Fee. *Discovering Biblical Equality*. Leicester: IVP, 2005.

Piper, John & Wayne Grudem. *Recovering Biblical Manhood and Womanhood: A Response to Evangelical Feminism*. Illinois: Crossway, 1991.

Simpson, Albert, B. *Christ in the Bible Series: Luke*. Harrisburg: Christian Publications, ND.

Spangler, Anne & Jean E. Syswerda. *Women of the Bible: A One Year Devotional Study of Women in the Bible*. Grand Rapids: Zondervan, 1999.

Spencer, Franklin, S. *Journeying Through Acts*. Massachusetts: Hendrickson, 2004.

Stott, John R. *The Message of Acts: To the Ends of the Earth*, Leicester: IVP, 1997.

Stuart, A. Moody. *The Three Marys*. Edinburgh: Banner of Truth, 1984.

Van Wijk-Bos, Johanna W.H. *Ruth and Esther: Women in Alien Lands.* Nashville: Abingdon Press, 2001.

Wiersbe, Warren, W. *Be Available: Judges.* Harpenden: Scripture Press Foundation, 1994.

Wilcock, Michael. *The Bible Speaks Today: The Message of Judges, Grace Abounding,* Leicester: IVP, 1992.

Wilkins, Michael J. *The New Application Commentary.* Grand Rapids: Zondervan, 2004.

Williams, David J. *The New International Bible Commentary: Acts.* Massachusetts: Hendrickson, 1999.

Willimon, William H. *Interpretation: Acts.* Atlanta: John Knox Press, 1988.

Winston, George & Dora Winston. *Recovering Biblical Ministry by Women.* Longwood: Xulon Press, 2003.

Younger, K. Lawson Jr. *The NIV Application Commentary: Judges/Ruth.* Grand Rapids: Zondervan, 2002.

Websites

Baker's Evangelical Dictionary of Theology, "Kinsman Redeemer," http://www.biblestudytools.com/dictionaries/bakers-evangelical-dictionary/kinsman-redeemer.html (accessed 4/01/2012).

Bible Bulletin Board, "Women of the Bible—Mary Magdalene: A Woman who was an adoring disciple (2000)," http://www.biblebb.com/files/kss/kss-mmag.htm   (accessed 14/07/2011).

Bible.org., "Yes, My Lord–The Story of Abraham and Sarah," http://bible.org/seriespage/yes-my-lord%E2%80%94-ithe-story-abraham-and-sarahi (accessed 13/07/2011).

Bible.org, "Be honest-The story of Ananias and Sapphira," http://bible.org/seriespage/be-honest (accessed 4/01/2012).

Biblos.com. Strong's Exhaustive Concordance *almanah,* http://concordances.org/hebrew/490.htm (accessed 4/01/2012).

Christian meaning of names, "Abigail," http://www.christianmeaningofnames.com/abigail (accessed 27/06/2011).

Global action on Aging, "The rights of Older People—African Perspectives, 1-15," www.globalaging.org/elderrights/world/2008/africa.pdf (accessed 27/07/2011)

The Church of God Daily Bible Study "Widows," http://www.keyway.ca/htm2006/20060222.htm (accessed 4/01/2012).

The Quote Garden, "Marriage Quotes," http://www.quotegarden.com/marriage.html (accessed 13/07/2011).

Unicef, "Basic education and gender equality—The Big Picture," http://www.unicef.org/education/index_bigpicture.html (accessed: 13/07/2011).

Women in the Bible.net, "Deborah, Her Story: Never Say Die," http://www.womeninthebible.net/1.8.Deborah_Jael.htm (accessed 4/01/2012).

Women in the Bible.net, "Ruth and Naomi: Loyalty and Love," http://www.womeninthebible.net/1.13.Ruth.htm (accessed 4/01/2012).

Women in the Bible.net, "Jezebel: Don't Mess with Me," http://www.womeninthebible.net/1.12.Jezebel.htm (accessed 4/01/2012).

---

¹ Cited by Allan Anderson, *An Introduction to Pentecostalism: Global Charismatic Christianity*, (Cambridge: University Press, 2004), 273.

² For further information on 'Jesus' treatment of women in the Bible' see Ronald W. Pierce, Rebecca Merrill Groothuis and Gordon D. Fee (eds.) *Discovering Biblical Equality*, (Leicester: IVP, 2005), 126-141.

³ *Ibid.,* 141.

⁴ Richard L. Strauss, *Yes, My Lord – The Story of Abraham and Sarah,* Bible.org http://bible.org/seriespage/yes-my-lord%E2%80%94-ithe-story-abraham-and-sarahi (13/07/2011).

⁵ Ronald A. Beers (Gen. ed.), *Life Application Study Bible: NIV,* (Grand Rapids: Zondervan, 1991), 2.

⁶ *Ibid.,* xv.

⁷ Strauss, *Yes, My Lord – The Story of Abraham and Sarah,* http://bible.org/seriespage/yes-my-lord%E2%80%94-ithe-story-abraham-and-sarahi

⁸ Nathaniel Hawthorne (American novelist) *The Quote Garden,* http://www.quotegarden.com/marriage.html (13/07/2011).

⁹ Gordon J. Wenham "Genesis", in *Eerdmans Commentary on the Bible,* eds. James J. G. Dunn and John W. Rogerson (Grand Rapids: Eerdmans, 2003), 51.

¹⁰ Elizabeth Fletcher, *Deborah, Her Story: Never Say Die,* Women in the Bible.net, http://www.womeninthebible.net/1.8.Deborah_Jael.htm (4/01/2012).

[11] Wayne Grudem (Gen. ed.) *ESV Study Bible* (Wheaton, Illinois: Crossway Bibles, 2008), 445.

[12] Michael Wilcock, *The Bible Speaks Today: The Message of Judges, Grace Abounding,* (Leicester: IVP, 1992), 60.

[13] K. Lawson Younger Jr. *The NIV Application Commentary: Judges/Ruth,* (Grand Rapids: Zondervan, 2002), 159.

[14] Warren W. Wiersbe, *Be Available: Judges* (Harpenden: Scripture Press Foundation, 1994), 42.

[15] Elizabeth Fletcher, *Deborah, Her Story: Never Say Die,* http://www.womeninthebible.net/1.8.Deborah_Jael.htm

[16] Gordon J. Keddie, *Even in Darkness* (Darlington: Evangelical Press, 1985), 53.

[17] Elizabeth Fletcher, *Ruth and Naomi: Loyalty and Love,* Women in the Bible.net, http://www.womeninthebible.net/1.13.Ruth.htm (4/01/2012).

[18] Beers, *Life Application Study Bible: NIV*, 421.

[19] ***Strong's Exhaustive Concordance*** *almanah*, Biblos.com. http://concordances.org/hebrew/490.htm (4/01/2012).

[20] Wayne Blank, *Widows, The Church of God Daily Bible Study,* http://www.keyway.ca/htm2006/20060222.htm (4/01/2012).

[21] Johanna W. H. Van Wijk-Bos, *Ruth and Esther: Women in Alien Lands,* (Nashville: Abingdon Press, 2001), 25.

[22] Younger Jr., *The NIV Life Application Commentary: Judges/Ruth,* 451.

[23] David Atkinson, *The Message of Ruth,* (Leicester: IVP, 1994), 27-

28.

²⁴ Stephen J. Bramer, "Kinsman Redeemer" in *Baker's Evangelical Dictionary of Theology,* http://www.biblestudytools.com/dictionaries/bakers-evangelical-dictionary/kinsman-redeemer.html (4/01/2012).

²⁵ Jean Syswerda, (Gen. ed.) *Women of Faith Study Bible: NIV,* (Grand Rapids: Zondervan, 2001), 805.

²⁶ Christian meaning of names 'Abigail,' http://www.christianmeaningofnames.com/abigail (27/06/2011).

²⁷ Beers, *Life Application Study Bible: NIV,* 427.

²⁸ Bruce C. Birch, "1 & 2 Samuel" in *The New Interpreters' Bible Commentary* Vol. 2, ed. Leander E. Keck (Nashville: Abingdon, 1998), 1166.

²⁹ Joyce Baldwin, *1 & 2 Samuel*, (Leicester: IVP, 1988), 147.

³⁰ Levenson cited by P. Kyle McCarter Jr. *1 Samuel: The Anchor Bible* (New York: Doubleday, 1980), 396.

³¹ Baldwin, *1 & 2 Samuel*, 149.

³² McCarter *1 Samuel*, 397.

³³ Baldwin, *1 & 2 Samuel*, 149.

³⁴ Mary J. Evans, *The Message of Samuel,* (Nottingham: IVP, 2004), 140.

³⁵ *Ibid.,* 141.

³⁶ Ralph W. Klein, *Word Biblical Commentary 10, 1 Samuel,* (Waco,

TX: Word Books, 1983), 250.

[37] Birch, "1 & 2 Samuel," in *The New Interpreters' Bible Commentary, Vol. II*, ed. Keck, 1164.

[38] Dale Ralph Davis, *1 Samuel: Looking on the Heart,* (Fearn: Christian Focus, 2000), 209.

[39] McCarter, *1 Samuel,* 398.

[40] Baldwin, *1 & 2 Samuel*, 150.

[41] McCarter, *1 Samuel*, 400.

[42] Baldwin, *1 & 2 Samuel*, 153-154.

[43] *Ibid.,* 151-152.

[44] Robert Laird Harris, Gleason Leonard Archer, Jr, & Bruce K. Waltke, *Theological Word Book of the Old Testament* (Chicago: Moody Press, 1980), 931.

[45] William D. Mounce, *Mounce's Complete Expository Dictionary of Old and New Testament Words*, (Grand Rapids: Zondervan, 2006), 503.

[46] J. Andrew Kirk, *Mission Under Scrutiny: Confronting Current Challenges,* (London: Darton, Longman & Todd, 2006) 132.

[47] Simon J. DeVries, *Word Biblical Commentary: 1 Kings,* (Waco Texas: Word Books, 1985), 204.

[48] Elizabeth Fletcher, *Jezebel: Don't Mess with Me,* http://www.womeninthebible.net/1.12.Jezebel.htm (4/01/2012).

[49] Syswerda, Women of Faith Study Bible, 1076.

[50] Beers, *Life Application Study Bible: NIV*, 543.

[51] Fletcher, *Jezebel: Don't Mess with Me*
http://www.womeninthebible.net/1.12.Jezebel.htm

[52] Musa Gotom, "1 and 2 Kings," in *Africa Bible Commentary,* ed. Tokunboh Adeyemo (Grand Rapids: Zondervan, 2006), 436.

[53] John Day, "Baal," in *The Anchor Bible Dictionary Vol.1,* ed. David Noel Freedman (New York: Doubleday, 1992), 547.

[54] Musa Gotom, "1 and 2 Kings," in *Africa Bible Commentary,* 441.

[55] Read more about this on Stepping Stones Nigeria, *Child Witches: The Issues,"* http://www.steppingstonesnigeria.org/witchcraft.html (13/07/2011).

[56] Mervin Breneman, *The New American Commentary: Ezra, Nehemiah, Esther,* (USA: Broadman & Holman, 1993), 315.

[57] Beers, *Life Application Study Bible: NIV,* 821.

[58] For more information on HIV/AIDS see Jean Garland & Dr. Mike Blyth, *AIDS is Real,* (Bukuru: Africa Christian Textbooks, 2005).

[59] Joyce G. Baldwin, *Esther: An Introduction and Commentary,* (Leicester: IVP, 1984), 69.

[60] Lois Semenye, "Esther," in *Africa Bible Commentary,* 563.

[61] Syswerda, *Women of Faith Study Bible,* 1645.

[62] Craig Evans, *Luke,* (Massachusetts: Hendrickson Publishers, 1990), 40.

[63] Darrell L. Bock, *Luke,* (Grand Rapids: Zondervan, 1996), 95.

⁶⁴ *Ibid.,* 98.

⁶⁵ Michael Bentley, *Saving a Fallen World,* (Darlington: Evangelical Press, 1992), 37.

⁶⁶ Dorothy Kelley Patterson & Rhonda Harrington Kelley (eds.) *Women's Evangelical Commentary: New Testament,* (Nashville: Broadman & Holman, 2006), 145.

⁶⁷Jody Kollapan, *The rights of Older People—African Perspectives, 1-15,* www.globalaging.org/elderrights/world/2008/africa.pdf (27/07/11).

⁶⁸ J. Ellsworth Kalas, *Strong Was Her Faith: Women of the New Testament,* (Nashville: Abingdon Press, 2007), 19.

⁶⁹ Kalas, *Strong Was Her Faith,* 17.

⁷⁰ Albert B. Simpson, *Christ in the Bible Series: Luke,* (Harrisburg, PA: Christian Pubs. Inc., ND), 17.

⁷¹ Kathryn Cappocia, *Women of the Bible—Mary Magdalene: A Woman who was an adoring disciple (2000),* http://www.biblebb.com/files/kss/kss-mmag.htm (14/07/2011).

⁷² Elisabeth Moltmann-Wendel, *The Women around Jesus,* (New York: Crossroad, 1996), 65.

⁷³ Beers, *Life Application Study Bible: NIV,* 1637; A. Moody Stuart, *The Three Marys,* (Edinburgh: Banner of Truth, 1984), 16.

⁷⁴ Stuart, *The Three Marys,* 20; Moltmann-Wendel, *The Women Around Jesus,* 64-67; Grudem, *ESV Study Bible,* 1967.

⁷⁵ Kalas, *Strong Was Her Faith,* 66.

⁷⁶ Michael J. Wilkins, *The NIV Application Commentary: Matthew,*

(Zondervan: Grand Rapids, 2004), 940.

[77] *Ibid.,* 911.

[78] Moltmann-Wendel, *The Women Around Jesus*, 64.

[79] Mounce, *Mounce's Complete Expository Dictionary*, 26.

[80] Wilkins, *The NIV Application Commentary: Matthew*, 942.

[81] Frank E. Gaebelein, (Gen. ed.) *The Expositor's Bible Commentary Vol. 9: John- Acts,* (Grand Rapids: Zondervan, 1984), 313.

[82] Beers, *Life Application Study Bible,* 1940.

[83] John R. W. Stott, *The Message of Acts: To the Ends of the Earth,* (Leicester: IVP, 1997), 109.

[84] Ajith Fernando, *The NIV Application Commentary: Acts,* (Grand Rapids: Zondervan, 1998), 196.

[85] Stott, *The Message of Acts*, 110.

[86] Mounce (ed.), *Mounce's Complete Expository Dictionary*, 348.

[87] Richard L. Strauss, *Be honest-The story of Ananias and Sapphira,* http://bible.org/seriespage/be-honest, (4/01/2012).

[88] Gaebelein, *Expositor's Bible Commentary: John-Acts,* 315.

[89] Gaebelein, *Expositor's Bible Commentary: John-Acts*, 382; Kalas, Strong Was Her Faith, 78-79.

[90] Beers, Life Application Study Bible, 1940.

[91] Kalas, Strong Was Her Faith, 81.

[92] I. Howard Marshall, The Acts of the Apostles: An Introduction and Commentary, (Leicester: IVP, 1999), 179.

[93] Kalas, *Strong Was Her Faith*, 83.

[94] Garland & Blyth, *Aids is Real and it's in our Church*, 16.

[95] William H. Willimon, *Interpretation: Acts*, (Atlanta: John Knox Press, 1988), 84.

[96] Kalas, *Strong Was Her Faith*, 80.

[97] Marshall, *Acts,* 179.

[98] Stott, *The Message of Acts,* 184.

[99] David J. Williams, *New International Bible Commentary: Acts,* (Massachusetts: Hendrickson, 1999), 182.

[100] William Neil, *The New Century Bible Commentary: The Acts of the Apostles*, (Grand Rapids: Eerdmans, 1986), 152.

[101] Syswerda, *Women of Faith Study Bible*, 2017.

[102] Beers, *Life Application Study Bible*, 1940.

[103] Stott, *The Message of Acts*, 263.

[104] Kalas, *Strong Was Her Faith*, 89.

[105] Franklin S. Spencer, *Journeying Through Acts,* (Massachusetts: Hendrickson, 2004), 174.

[106] Marshall, *Acts,* 267.

[107] Kalas, *Strong Was Her Faith*, 90.

[108] Leander E. Keck (ed.), *The New Interpreter's Bible Vol. X,* (Nashville: Abingdon Press, 2002), 235.

¹⁰⁹ Kalas, *Strong Was Her Faith*, 91.

¹¹⁰ Paul Mumu Kisau, "Acts," in *Africa Bible Commentary,* 1329.

¹¹¹ Graham Kendrick, "From Heaven You Came" (162) in Peter Horrobin and Greg Leavers (comp.) *Complete Mission Praise,* (London: Harper Collins, 2005).

¹¹² Anne Spangler and Jean E. Syswerda, *Women of the Bible: A One Year Devotional Study of Women in the Bible,* (Grand Rapids: Zondervan, 1999), 420.

¹¹³ Beers, *Life Application Study Bible,* 1940.

¹¹⁴ Fernando, *The NIV Application Commentary: Acts*, 491.

¹¹⁵ Stott, *The Message of Acts*, 294.

¹¹⁶ Fernando, *The NIV Application Commentary: Acts*, 496.

¹¹⁷ Stott, *The Message of Acts*, 297.

¹¹⁸ Amy G. Oden, *And you welcomed me,* (Nashville: Abingdon Press, 2001), 13 & 14.

¹¹⁹ Michele Hershberger, *A Christian View of Hospitality,* (Scottdale: Herald Press, 1999), 31.

¹²⁰ Stott, *The Message of Acts*, 296.

¹²¹ Unicef: *Basic education and gender equality—The Big Picture,* http://www.unicef.org/education/index_bigpicture.html, (Accessed: 13/07/2011).

¹²² Martin Smith, "Men of faith, rise up and sing," (1094) in Peter

Horrobin and Greg Leavers (comp.) *Complete Mission Praise,* (London: Harper Collins, 2005).

www.ingramcontent.com/pod-product-compliance
Lightning Source LLC
Chambersburg PA
CBHW071402150726
48000CB00001B/124